Arthur Tappan Pierson

Shall We Continue in Sin?

A vital question for believers answered in the Word of God, the substance of addresses delivered in Great Britain and Ireland in 1896

Arthur Tappan Pierson

Shall We Continue in Sin?
A vital question for believers answered in the Word of God, the substance of addresses delivered in Great Britain and Ireland in 1896

ISBN/EAN: 9783337325053

Printed in Europe, USA, Canada, Australia, Japan

Cover: Foto ©Lupo / pixelio.de

More available books at **www.hansebooks.com**

SHALL WE CONTINUE IN SIN?

A VITAL QUESTION FOR BELIEVERS
ANSWERED IN THE WORD OF GOD

THE SUBSTANCE OF ADDRESSES DELIVERED IN
GREAT BRITAIN AND IRELAND IN 1896

BY

ARTHUR T. PIERSON

NEW YORK
THE BAKER & TAYLOR COMPANY
5 AND 7 EAST SIXTEENTH STREET

COPYRIGHT, 1897, BY
THE BAKER & TAYLOR COMPANY

TROW DIRECTORY
PRINTING AND BOOKBINDING COMPANY
NEW YORK

To

REV. EVAN H. HOPKINS,
OF LONDON, ENGLAND,

And to those who with him are seeking to lead God's people out of the wilderness into the Land of Promise, and teach them "The Law of Liberty in the Spiritual Life," this little book is dedicated by his friend, the Author, with deep affection, and gratitude for the blessing received through his testimony to the fulness of Blessing which is in Christ Jesus

CONTENTS

	PAGE
INTRODUCTORY,	9
I. JUDICIAL UNION WITH CHRIST,	13
II. VITAL UNION WITH CHRIST,	32
III. PRACTICAL UNION WITH CHRIST,	47
IV. ACTUAL UNION WITH CHRIST,	60
V. MARITAL UNION WITH CHRIST,	79
VI. SPIRITUAL UNION WITH CHRIST,	91
VII. ETERNAL UNION WITH CHRIST,	107

SHALL WE CONTINUE IN SIN?

INTRODUCTORY

THE Bible is the most practical of all books. It is a fact, both curious and significant, that, somewhere, in the word of God, we may find at least once, a full if not an exhaustive discussion of each particular matter, which has close relations to man's salvation and sanctification.

For example, the value and excellence of the Law of God is treated in Psalm cxix.; the fact of Vicarious Atonement, in Isaiah liii.; the nature of the Kingdom of God and its true subjects, in Matthew v., vi., vii.; the Beauty of Charity, in I. Corinthians xiii.; the Resurrection of the Dead, in I. Corinthians xv.; the Principles of Christian Giving, in II. Corinthians viii., ix., etc. The person and work of the Holy Spirit, in John xiv., xv., xvi. The present Rest of Faith, in Hebrews iii., iv. The mischief of an untamed tongue, in James iii. And so here, in three chapters, in Romans vi., vii., viii., we have the Duty and Privilege of non-continuance in Sin set before us with a clearness and fulness which make all other discussion of the subject comparatively needless.

We cannot mistake the subject here treated. The sixth chapter opens with the plain question: *Shall we continue in sin?* a question substantially repeated in verse 15, Shall we sin? and in chapter vii. 7, Is the Law Sin? In all three cases the answer is a short, energetic, and most emphatic " God forbid ! " The very thought is to be put away as a fatal snare to the soul, as when Christ said to Satan, "Get thee hence ! " Nothing could more clearly teach that continuance in sinning is to be regarded by every true child of God as both needless and wrong. The doctrine of sinlessness is not here taught, but of not continuing in sin. Being without sin, and not going on in sin, are two quite different things.*

---

* Comp. 1 John i. 8—ii. 1. Also Dr. Handley Moule, in a letter quoted in the Homiletic Review. September, 1896, p. 242.

" But I come to speak briefly of the limits.

" I will not dwell upon them, but I must indicate them. I mean, of course, not limits in our aims, for there must be none, nor limits in divine grace itself, for there are none, but limits, however caused, in the actual attainment by us of Christian holiness.

" Here I hold, with absolute conviction, alike from the experience of the church and from the infallible Word, that, in the mystery of things, there will be limits to the last, and very humbling limits, very real fallings short. To the last it will be a sinner that walks with God. To the last will ' abide in the regenerate ' (art. ix.) that strange tendency, that ' mind of the

Thus does Paul introduce a discussion of this theme which occupies three chapters of this epistle; for there seems to be no break in the continuity of the argument, until the close of the eighth chapter, where, manifestly, he closes the discussion of this subject and enters upon another. To examine this topic, therefore, and get the whole force of the divine argument, we need to regard these three chapters as a whole, and follow from step to step, till we reach the grand climax.

One great thought runs like a thread of gold through the whole of this process of reasoning, namely: that *the disciple's security for non-continuance in sinning is found in his Union with the Lord Jesus Christ*. This, which in previous chapters is presented as the sole ground of *Justification*, is now presented also as the sole basis and hope of *Sanctification:* as Christ does away with the *penalty* for sin by His death, so by His Life He puts an end to its *power* over the true believer.

flesh,' which eternal grace can wonderfully deal with, but which is a tendency still.

"To the last, the soul's acceptance before the Judge is wholly and only in the righteousness, the merits, of Christ.

"To the last, if we say we have no sin, we deceive ourselves. In the pure, warm sunshine of the Father's smile shed upon him, the loving and willing child will yet say, 'Enter not into judgment with thy servant.' Walking in the light as He is in the light, having fellowship with him, and He with us, we yet need to the last the blood of Calvary, the blood of propitiation, to deal with sin."

As these chapters are carefully examined, this union of the disciple with Christ appears to be considered in a *seven-fold aspect* which, for convenience sake, we may indicate or designate by seven words which, without, perhaps, being scrupulously exact, may serve simply as so many landmarks to outline the grand divisions of the argument: Judicial, Vital, Practical, Actual, Marital, Spiritual, and Eternal.

I

JUDICIAL UNION WITH CHRIST

THE first aspect of this union of the believer with Christ is the *Judicial*. This belongs first in logical order as basis of all the rest. This word, Judicial, is a *legal* term, having reference to the act or decision of a judge in a court of law. It is peculiar in this, that it has no necessary reference to, or connection with, the *actual character* or even *guilt* of the accused party. A judicial decision concerns one question only, namely, the claim of the law upon him and the jurisdiction of the court over him. A man may be actually a transgressor, and yet for some reason be not amenable to a legal penalty. There may be some technicality, under cover of which he escapes, or some sovereign act of mercy removing him from the control of the court, or some interposition of a third party mediating between him and exact justice. In either case, without regard to his essential merit or the moral desert of his acts, the judge pronounces him acquitted, in effect legally innocent. A judicial decision, therefore, refers to *standing* rather than *state;* it is a question of exposure to penalty, not of essential character or moral desert.

For example, in the former days when bankruptcy was treated as a crime and debtors were imprisoned, a man's debts were sometimes discharged by another, and he was consequently released. He might have been careless and even dishonest in the use of funds, and deserving of punishment as a moral offender, but the only question before the court would be, are his debts paid? and if so the judicial decision would be that he was a free man.

A case recently occurred in British Courts, where a man was sued for breach of promise. It was a case of flagrant wrong. The man had led the woman to believe that he would marry her, and his whole course with her justified such expectation; but no proof could be adduced that any explicit pledge had been given, and he was acquitted, although he was, in fact, a seducer and betrayer.

These two examples, respectively, illustrate the effect of the interposition of a third party, or of the absence of technical proof, in freeing an accused party from the penalty of law. As to the effect of a sovereign act of clemency, that may be seen in Pilate's release of Barabbas, or in any act of pardon issued by proper magisterial authority.

We have thus given three examples of judicial acquittal:

1. On the basis of a technicality: Breach of promise.
2. On the basis of a Sovereign Act: Pardon of State prisoners as on the accession or coronation of a King.
3. On the basis of human interposition: Bankruptcy.

Illustrations might be multiplied, were it needful, to show this principle, but these suffice to make clear that a judicial decision has reference only to a man's attitude before the law, to his legal standing and not his moral state, his liability or exposure to penalty, and not his inherent character and actual desert; and we have been thus careful to define the term judicial, because the whole system of redemption rests upon this basis, that God has made a provision whereby He can judicially acquit a guilty sinner. With this great fact and thought the whole of the first part of the Epistle to the Romans is mainly occupied.

First, the Apostle proves that all men, Gentiles and Jews alike, are guilty before God. With different degrees of light and revelation of His will, they have all alike sinned and come short of the Glory of God. And by an irresistible argument he reaches this conclusion, that every mouth is stopped and all the world becomes guilty before God (iii. 19). There is no man who is not a sinner, and a sinner without excuse. And he adds, "Therefore, by the deeds of the law there shall no flesh be justified in his sight."

Here we come to another legal term which it is necessary for us to understand : *Justified*. It is not equivalent to *just*, but rather in contrast with it. The word, just, refers to character; justified, to standing. If an unjust man is judicially acquitted he is, so far as the law is concerned, justified; that is, accounted and treated as just or righteous.

The Problem of Redemption was this; to justify the sinner without justifying his sin, to save him from legal penalty and yet save God from compromise and complicity with his guilt. Justice demanded the exaction of penalty in the interest of law and perfect government; mercy yearned to rescue the offender in the interests of love and divine fatherhood. The problem was so perplexing that only Infinite Wisdom and grace together were equal to its solution. Now that it is solved, it may seem simple, as it is easy to unlock the most complicated lock when you have the key that belongs to it ; but, if that problem had been originally submitted to the united wisdom of all human philosophers and wise men, it would still remain unsolved.

We can plainly see some of the difficulties that entered into the case. There was no question that all men were sinners, sinners against a righteous God and a perfect law, and it is equally evident that the sanctions of government must be maintained; for the moment that the certainty that every transgression and disobedience will receive its just recompense of reward no longer exists, good government is not only in peril—it has absolutely *ceased*. If God would save the sinner from his just punishment, He must not do it at the expense of His own law or His own holiness. Any judge in any court that allows laxity in administering justice sets a premium upon crime. Chief Justice Hale used to say, "When I feel myself swayed by the impulses of mercy toward an offender, let me remember that there is a mercy due unto my country."

The root idea of the gospel is that, by the substitution of Christ for the sinner before the law, in a perfect life of obedience and a death of vicarious suffering, the ends of the law and of justice were so answered as that God could judicially acquit the sinner and yet not tarnish the glory of his own perfection. To get hold of that truth is the beginning of our education in the School of Christ, for it is the first lesson in Redemption.

We can all see that several ends might be answered by the punishment of sin in the person of the actual transgressor. For example, it would serve:

1. To magnify the Law and make it honorable.
2. To uphold the sanctions of perfect government.

3. To visit just penalty upon transgressors.
4. To exhibit the essential guilt and ill desert of sin.
5. To warn and deter other offenders.
6. To indicate and vindicate the character of God.
7. To discriminate between the righteous and the wicked.

Now were not all these ends met in the atoning work of our Lord Jesus Christ? Transgression was visited with a penalty which also exhibited the deformity and enormity of sin; and an eternal lesson was taught the universe which may, to an extent now inconceivable by us, warn and deter other creatures of God from evil-doing; and it has been shown that the Law and government of God will be upheld at any cost, and that in the great God Himself there is infinite abhorrence of sin.

Of course our point of prospect is limited; there may be other purposes answered in Christ's substitution of which we have now neither knowledge nor notion; but we can see enough already to feel moved like Paul himself to exclaim, "O the depth of the riches both of the wisdom and knowledge of God! How unsearchable are His Judgments and His ways past finding out!" Rom. xi. 33.

The fact, declared in this Epistle, whether or not we are equal to the divine philosophy of it, is, that "now the Righteousness of God apart from the law is manifested; even the Righteousness of

God which is by faith of Jesus Christ, unto all, and upon all them that believe," etc. Chap. iii. 21-26.

Let us learn this by heart, for it is the very sum and substance of the whole mystery of Redemption : All have sinned and come short of His glory, and therefore there is no hope of justification through the law, which can only make us more and more terribly conscious of sin and guilt. But God has set forth Christ Jesus to be a Propitiation for our sins, and we may be justified freely by His grace through faith in His blood.

Now notice where lies the emphasis of this whole passage : God hath set forth his Atoning Son, not to declare His indifference to sin and His laxity in pardoning, but "*to declare His righteousness*"— even in the remission of sin. And Paul repeats this that it may more deeply engrave itself on our minds—to declare I say at this time His Righteousness : *that He might be just and the Justifier of him which believeth in Jesus.* In one word the purpose and perfection of this atoning work is that it makes it possible for a Just and Holy God to remain perfectly just and holy, and yet not only pardon a sinner but account him just, that is, *judicially* acquit him and give him the standing of an innocent party.

The natural and carnal heart wars against even the grace of God, too proud to submit to being saved in God's way, because all boasting is excluded. And so men find fault with the very love that seeks to find provision in atonement. The sinner dares to criticise grace and declares that it is impossible for an innocent party to take the place of the guilty, or for a judicial acquittal to be justly pronounced in the transgressor's case. And yet the principle of vicarious substitution is not wholly unknown even in human affairs. It is a story, told of Bronson Alcott, that, when obliged to administer a bodily chastisement upon a disobedient school-boy, his older brother who was present asked that he might receive the flogging in place of the offender. And Professor Alcott put the question to the school, whether the laws which the boys had themselves framed would be sufficiently honored by such substitution, and they consented ; so that he actually whipped the older brother in place of the younger transgressor, and with a profound impression on the school-boys both as to the dignity of Law and the unselfishness of Love and Mercy. Whether or not the incident be authentic, it serves as an illustration.

Enough has been written perhaps to introduce us to the great thought first presented in this sixth chapter of Romans. When Paul asks, shall we continue in sin ? his first reply is, How shall we that have died to sin live any longer therein ! Know ye not that so many of us as were baptized into Jesus Christ were baptized into His death ? Therefore we are buried with him by baptism into death. Here three affirmations meet us: first we *have died* to sin; second, so many as were baptized into Jesus Christ were *baptized into his death;* third, by such baptism we were *buried with him* into death. In other words, there has been on the part of every believer, a death unto sin; and a burial with Christ in the sepulchre; and that death and burial are expressed, confessed and symbolized in baptism.

It is perfectly plain that these words can be understood only *judicially*. We are all of us conscious of no such actual identification with Christ in death and burial. We have never yet really died or been laid in the grave. The only way to interpret these words is to interpret them, not as expressing a historical fact, but a judicial act, something counted or reckoned or imputed to our account by the sovereign mercy and grace of God. That they are so to be interpreted is plain from the whole argument preceding. The first direct mention of a judicial righteousness found in the New Testament is in the opening chapters of this Epistle. The germ of it is in the gospels and the Acts, but the germ comes to its growth and plain exhibition here, as we have seen in Romans iii. 19–28. There we are plainly taught that God has devised a plan for human redemption, whereby He reckons the believing and penitent sinner so one with Christ that His obedience is imputed to the sinner as his own and His atoning suffering is reckoned as the sinner's own expiation or satisfaction of the legal claim and penalty. Here we are first introduced to the full meaning of that truth of which the whole Bible is at once the miracle and the parable, that the unity of a believing sinner with an atoning Saviour is first of all a *judicial* one, reckoned such, apart from all our legal obedience, and our undeserving character, by the infinite grace of God. This is the fundamental fact and truth of redemption, and faith in it is fundamental to our salvation. The believer is *in Jesus*, in the sight of God, and is so judged and acquitted as clothed with God's righteousness.

Paul, moreover, shows that this doctrine of Righteousness imputed on account of faith, is no new doctrine, but pervades the old Covenant as well as the new, for he refers back to Abraham, the father of the faithful, and to that grand verse in Genesis (xv. 6) where for the first time in the Word of God we meet these three words in conjunction—believed, counted, and Righteousness. There it is declared that Abraham believed in Jehovah and He counted, or imputed it unto him for righteousness. That verse becomes the key to the Epistles to the Romans and to the Galatians, and to the Epistle of James, thus linking old and new Testaments together.* The doctrine thus found in the "Law" is also found in "the Psalms" and the "Prophets." †

* Rom. iv. 1-5. Gal. iii. 6. James ii. 23.
† Compare Psalm xxxii. 1, 2, and Habakkuk ii. 4.

How far this acquittal of the sinner is judicial, based on the ground of imputation, not actual righteousness in the sinner, is plain from Rom. iv. 17—where we are told that God quickeneth the dead and *calleth those things which be not as though they were*. God in justifying sinners actually counts them righteous when they are not—does not impute sin where sin actually exists, and does impute righteousness where it does not exist. Abraham, because he had God's *promise*, counted as done what seemed impossible as well as unreal; and God honored such faith by in turn counting as existing in Abraham a righteousness which was not his. The believer counts God able to make him alive with His own life and holy with His own holiness. God in turn counts the sinner now dead *in* sin to be dead *to* sin and alive to God, counts him as righteous, and then proceeds to *make* him what he at first only *reckons* him to be. Comp. Romans iv. 4–8, 17, 21, 22.

This plan of salvation is further unfolded in the fifth chapter. Being thus justified by faith we have peace with God—all controversy between us and Him is forever over—and all conflict with His perfect law and holy government. We were "without strength" to help ourselves but He laid help on One who is mighty to save. We were sinners and Christ died in our stead; we were enemies and by his death the enmity was done away in reconciliation: chap. v. 6–8. So that, where sin abounded and reigned unto death, grace much more abounds and reigns unto eternal life. However we may quarrel with God's plan of salvation there is no doubt about the plan as here taught.

What pregnant words then are these seven! "Buried with Him by baptism into death."

Burial implies death and death implies previous life.

"With Him" implies that all this experience of life, death and burial is through our identification with Him, our Lord Jesus.

"By baptism" implies that the act whereby this identification is both symbolized and exhibited is baptism.

It now becomes clear in what sense we have died to sin—been buried with Christ and baptized into his death—*these become facts* by a *judicial construction*. Faith makes us one with Jesus Christ, so that, in God's sight, what is literally and actually true of Him, becomes judicially, representatively, constructively, true of us. We died when he died; we were buried when he was buried; and as many of us as have been baptized into Christ have been baptized into His death, that is, our baptism was the confession of our identity with Him, and our symbolic putting on of Christ. As the mutual clasping of hands or exchange of rings in marriage is the expression and confession and symbolism of the union of holy wedlock; as the taking off of the shoe was the confession of a holy place whereon one must walk softly and reverently with God; as the bowing of the body and bending of the knee are the expression of worship and spiritual prostration before God; so, to go down into a watery grave, as Christ did, expresses our faith in and following of Him—in His death and burial.*

Thus we touch the very heart of the gospel mystery, our identity by faith with the Son of God. And we touch also that kindred mystery of

---

* It is surprising what a consensus of opinion there is on this subject among the most devout commentators, see Vaughan on Romans, pp. 117, 118.

"All christians died when Christ died. That is the date, for all, of that death which is their life. But the personal appropriation of this death with Christ is later in time. It comes only with faith. Baptism (in case of a penitent and believing convert) was the moment of the individual incorporation. *We were baptized into Christ*, Acts 2, 38.

"We were buried then with him, by means of that baptism, into that death. In other words, our baptism was a sort of funeral; a solemn act of consigning us to that death of Christ in which we are made one with Him, and with this object: not that we might remain dead, but that we might rise with Him from death, experience (even in this world) the power of His resurrection, and live the life we now live in the flesh as men who have already died and risen again."

Also, Handley G. C. Moule, on Romans, p. 164.

"For if we became vitally connected, He with us, and we with Him, by the likeness of His death, by the baptismal plunge, symbol and seal of our faith-union with the buried sacrifice, why we shall be vitally connected with Him by the likeness also of His Resurrection, by the baptismal emergence, the Son of *Man*. He was Goël—the Redeemer—and a Redeemer must not only have power to redeem, by being lifted above the sin and corruption of the human race, but must have the right to redeem by being let down to the level of the race he sought to save. And so, in redeeming man, God must be manifest in the flesh. He must have the right to redeem by being identified with our humanity. The Son of God must become Son of Man. Hence Christ is called *the Second Man and the Last Adam*. 1 Cor. xv. 45, 47.

Observe, not the Second Man only, as in verse 47, but the *Last* Man or Adam—for this excludes any succession. We can understand the *last* Adam only by understanding the *first*. Who was the first Adam but the *Judicial Head* of the race he represented? Whatever may be our theological definition of our relation to Adam, the practical fact is that he *stood for us* and when he fell, we fell. He could transmit to his descendants no higher nature than his own, and so it is significantly said, that he begat a son in his own likeness. His own nature being fallen, he transmitted a fallen nature with its proneness to sin, and its exposure to pains and penalties. As he had lost his original estate,

---

symbol and seal of our faith-union with our risen Lord and so with His risen power."

Let it be remembered that the comments and the paraphrase above quoted, are from two of the leading evangelical clergymen of the Anglican Church.

his children could inherit only his moral bankruptcy and ruin ; and, as he had forfeited his right to the tree of life, his offspring find the cherubim with the flaming sword, still guarding the way, until we come by a new and living way, through the rent vail of Christ's crucified body.

Christ is therefore, as the Last Adam, what the first Adam was, the representative of the race. By blood and birth we were all identified with Adam ; by the faith in the blood that atones and by the new birth of the Spirit, we become identified with the Last Adam. We exchange the standing of sinners for the standing of saints, the bankruptcy of sin for the riches of holiness, and the forfeited right to the Tree of Life for the full and eternal enjoyment of all sacramental privilege. Rev. xxii. 1-14, R. V.

The most precious *names* applied to Christ are more or less a commentary on this most comprehensive title, the Last Adam. He is the Good Shepherd, so identified with the sheep that by his death he purchases their salvation from death. He is the Vine, so identified with the branches that by His life they receive life, strength, growth and power to bear fruit. He is the Foundation, the very basis, so identified with the building that every believer as a living stone both rests upon Him and is cemented to Him and built up with Him into one building or Temple of God and habitation of God through the Spirit. He is the Bridegroom, so one with the bride that she is reckoned part of Him, they twain being one flesh. He is the Head and we are members of His body and cannot be separated from Him, so identified with Him that all life, growth, sustenance, increase, depend on the union.

Hence we can understand how God reckons us to have died and been buried when He died and was buried. Judicially it is true, for what happens to our Great Representative is true of all whom he represents. We are not surprised then when we find, on the careful study of the New Testament, that this conception of our Judicial Union with Christ not only pervades all its teaching but is the interpreting Key to His life; all that He did and suffered as the Son of Man was *typical* and *representative* of the whole body of believers. In this sixth of Romans five words are used, all of them representative: "died," "buried," "risen," "planted," "crucified." All are declared to be applicable to us as believers. And when we turn to the Epistle to the Colossians this same thought is further expanded. Compare Coloss. ii. 10-13; iii. 1-4.

Here the great phrase is one of two words: IN HIM. He is the Head, and what is true of the Head is true of the body. Here seven terms are used to express this unity or identity—in Him and with Him it is declared that we are *circumcised, buried, risen, quickened, seated,* our life *hid* in God and to *appear* when He appears.

These seven phrases suggest that His whole life as Son of Man and Last Adam, was representative and typical; and that its full explanation can be found only in its representative character; that is, every great event or experience had reference to the body of which He is Head—the race of which He is the Last Adam.

In that career of Christ there are at least fifteen grand and salient points: His Birth or Incarnation, Presentation and Circumcision, Baptism, Anointing, Temptation, Passion, Crucifixion, Burial, Quickening, Resurrection, Forty days of Resurrection Walk, Ascension, Session at God's right hand and Hidden Life of Intercession, and final Reappearance. Every one of these is a typical fact, as will appear if we examine scripture. Hence the force of those constantly recurring phrases: in Him, by Him, for Him, through Him, with Him, etc.

His miraculous Birth was a type of our new birth from above whereby we enter the kingdom, not by a natural, but by a supernatural process.

His circumcision, the type of the putting off the body of the sins of the flesh. Col. ii. 11.

His presentation in the temple, of our self-offering to God. Rom. xii. 1.

His Baptism, of our Confession of Him as Saviour and Lord—the answer of a good conscience toward God. 1 Pet. iii. 21.

His Temptation, of our Conflict with and Conquest over Satan. Jas. iv. 7; 1 John iv. 4.

His Anointing, of our Reception of Holy Ghost indwelling and power. 1 John ii. 20–27.

His Passion, of our entire Surrender to the Will of God even unto death. Heb. xii. 4, 5.

His Crucifixion, of our death unto the penalty and guilt of sin. Gal. ii. 20.

His Burial, of our leaving in His sepulchre all corruption of the old man. Col. iii. 9.

His Resurrection, of our rising into newness of life. Col. iii. 1.

His Quickening, of our being pervaded by the life and power of God. Col. ii. 13.

His Forty Days of resurrection life and power correspond to our complete walk with God after regeneration. Rom. viii. 4, 5.

His Session at God's Right Hand, to our present life of privilege. Col. iii. 1, 2.

His Hidden Life, to our secret incorporation unto Him. Col. iii. 3.

His Intercession, to our identity with him in mediation. Heb. x. 19–21.

His Coming Again, to our final resurrection and revelation. Coloss. iii. 4.

This analogy might be indefinitely expanded and illustrated.

Note, for instance, the main incidents of His supernatural birth; "the Holy Ghost shall come upon thee and the power of the highest shall overshadow thee; therefore also that holy thing which shall be born of thee shall be called the Son of

God." And Mary's Answer: "Behold the handmaid of the Lord! be it unto me according to thy Word." In His Temptation the Prince of this World is Judged, and Satan bruised under our feet. Rom. xvi. 20. Anointing, poured on the Head, reaching all the members and to the skirts of the robe. Psalm cxxxiii.

To sum up then: In Him the believer finds himself born anew in a supernatural birth, realizes complete self-offering, and renunciation of sin, confessing his faith, receiving the anointing of the Spirit, meeting and overcoming the Tempter, bearing his sin in expiation of penalty; his old man is buried and left in the grave, the new man assumed, the whole inner life quickened; a perpetual walking with God, an ascension above earth and a session at God's right hand, a hidden life of privilege and intercession, losing even life in unselfish ministry, and a coming manifestation in glory and complete vindication and reward, become his.

This being the foundation truth of the whole scheme of Redemption, the two sacraments—all Christ left behind as memorials—both represent it: Baptism is *our entering* into Christ.

The Lord's Supper, *His Entering* unto us.

II

VITAL UNION WITH CHRIST

"THAT, Like as Christ was raised up from the dead by the glory of the Father, even so we also should walk in newness of Life." Chap. vi. 4–11. Comp. 2 Cor. xiii. 4.

From identification with Jesus in Death and Burial, we pass now rapidly to identification with him by Quickening and Resurrection. In this section of the argument, again we meet certain significant phrases on which the argument turns; the meaning of which we need to apprehend and master, even to the nicest shades of difference and distinction, for the Divine Artist used no colors, or shades of color, without discrimination:

1. Christ was *raised up* from the dead by the glory of the Father.

2. *Planted together* in the likeness of His resurrection.

3. Our old man is crucified with Him that the body of sin *might be destroyed*.

4. That henceforth we *should not serve sin*.

5. We believe that we shall also *live with Him*.
6. Death hath *no more dominion* over Him.
7. In that He liveth, He *liveth unto God*.

Here are six or seven phrases, no two alike, all expressing some new phase of our oneness with the *Risen Lord*, as before with the *Crucified* Christ. As nearly as we can discern the nice distinctions, they may be indicated as follows:

1. The believer is in Christ divinely quickened, or made alive;
2. He is permitted to share in the likeness of His Resurrection.
3. The Body of Sin is to be regarded as destroyed in His grave.
4. Henceforth the believer is not to be the slave of sin.
5. Out of Christ's grave is to come a new Life with Him.
6. Resurrection implies deliverance from the dominion of death.
7. Our new Life is to be a Life unto God.

Taken together, these thoughts constitute a body of truth that is so wondrously complete, that nothing can be added to it; and so divinely uplifting that it should make continuance in sinning impossible. Let us seek to get at least a glimpse of the meaning of some of these marvellous expressions.

1. Christ was raised up from the dead by the glory of the Father.

The grandeur of Christ's Resurrection, both in

itself and as a type of the believer's new life, no mortal mind has ever yet conceived. It is made in the New Testament, both the crowning miracle of all miracles and the crowning proof of Christ's deity, while it becomes henceforth God's new unit of measurement as to what He can and will accomplish in and for the believer.

It is the crowning miracle, for it embraces in itself all others. We see Him giving sight to blind eyes, hearing to deaf ears, speech to the dumb, power to palsied limbs and withered members : have we ever thought how in his own Resurrection all these were included? The eyes that were blind, the ears that were deaf, the limbs that were palsied and withered in death, received respectively sight, hearing, strength, and health in one simultaneous and supreme act. It was the crowning proof, sign, and seal of His Messiahship, in which He was declared to be the Son of God, with power by the Spirit of Holiness. Rom. i. 4. Consider how he was thrice dead—dead by crucifixion, with pierced hands and feet; dead by the spear thrust, which cleft his heart in twain ; dead by the temporary enswathement, which wrapped even his head and excluded breath even had he not otherwise been dead. Was there ever a more stupendous exhibition of divine power, attesting God's own direct working, than when that dead body awoke, arose, emerged from the embalming cloths—leaving them behind as a butterfly sloughs off its cocoon

—got up from its bed of stone, and stood and walked, and went forth from the sepulchre?

And now, henceforth, whenever the believer would know how much God is able and willing to accomplish for him, in answer to the prayer of faith, and because of his identification by faith with the crucified and risen Saviour, he has only to consider what God wrought in Christ when he raised him from the dead, and set him at his own right hand in the heavenlies. In the Old Testament God's unit of measurement is what He did for his people in bringing them out of the land of Egypt. Micah vii. 15. That deliverance included at least three things, all miracles of power and grace: first, the exemption from death, of the bloodstained houses; second, the defiance of the law of gravitation, in making the waters a wall; and third, the overthrow of all foes in the Red Sea. In the New Testament, the unit of measurement is a new one, according to the working of His mighty power, which He wrought in Christ when He raised Him from the dead, etc. Eph. i. 20.

This again includes three things, singularly correspondent to the other three—exemption from wrath on the part of every blood-sprinkled soul; defiance of gravitation in the ascension of Christ, and overthrow of all hostile principalities and powers, in Christ's session at God's Right Hand.

When we look at the power of sin over us and ask how it can be broken; when, in despair of all self-help and self-conquest, we cry out, who shall deliver me from the body of this death? the answer is, Trust in the living God who raised Him from the dead. The same power that wrought in Christ works in every new born soul. The struggles of the unbeliever against sin are comparatively fruitless and hopeless, and the efforts even of the regenerate man are unsuccessful, so long as he attempts to vanquish sin by his own resolve or power. But the believer must remember that in the Resurrection of Christ he receives life, and life stands for vitality, ability, energy, power. Before, he was dead in trespasses and sins, and death means helplessness, powerlessness, despair. In Christ he can do all things, while without Christ he can do nothing. The moment he understands and realizes his new *gift of life* in Christ's Resurrection he knows that, while so one with Jesus, the same works which were possible to Christ become possible to himself. This is the wonderful truth taught throughout the New Testament.

An illustration of this may be found in the familiar fact about the magnet. It has a mysterious life, the power of which can be communicated. For example, if you take a piece of common iron and allow it to be attracted to the magnet, it becomes attached to it, becomes itself magnetic, and while so held fast by the magnet attracts the iron or steel filings as the magnet does, but when severed from the magnet has no such attractive power. "Apart from me," says Christ, "ye can do nothing." But the moment Christ lays hold upon you, and His life is imparted to you, His works become possible to you.

We have found a second phrase here which teaches us that the believer shares in the likeness of his resurrection. This, of course, finds its completeness only in the final resurrection of saints. Yet, as Paul is here treating of our non-continuance in sin, there must be a larger sense in which we are *now* permitted to share in the similitude of His resurrection. Paul, writing to the Philippians, expresses his willingness to renounce all gains as losses, and all advantage as refuse, that he may know the power of Christ's resurrection. What is that power, but the power *over death*, the power that defies corruption, that releases from the bondage of death, and sets the dead free to live and move and have being? And what is the power of Christ's resurrection, as now enjoyed by the true believer, but the power over sin, which is death, the power that defies corruption longer to hold us in bondage, and makes us free men in Christ Jesus, with capacity to serve God in newness of life?

Resurrection was to Christ deliverance from all further liability or possibility of death; death hath no more dominion over Him. And this constitutes our Risen Saviour the first begotten from the dead, and the first fruits of them that slept.

There had been other revivals, resuscitations or restorations of the dead, but never a *resurrection* proper till He rose; for all others, such as Jairus's daughter, the son of the widow of Nain, and Lazarus, rose to die again—but Christ, being raised from the dead, *dieth no more.*

We ought to get hold of this great thought, for the thought itself is a deliverance, that by faith united to Christ, I *now* partake in the power and privilege of His resurrection. The spirit of Holiness who raised Him from the dead, henceforth to be free of all dominion of death, dwells in and works in me as a believer, and assures to me deliverance from the power of the sin that works death and is death.

How strongly does the Apostle state the purpose and effect of such identity with the Risen Lord, that the body of sin should be destroyed, that henceforth we should not serve sin. This language cannot well be mistaken. We are to regard the Body of Sin as destroyed in the grave of Christ, and left behind there, that henceforth we should be free from its dominion, delivered from the bondage of corruption, no more to be slaves of sin.

We are therefore to think of Christ's death as our death, His burial as our burial, His rising as our rising. We go into the grave with Him but not to stay there. His grave is the place of our burial, as the ground is the grave of the seed; but burial is in order to resurrection, as the burial of the seed is in order to germination and harvest.

Andrew Murray has beautifully said that the believer is to remember that the very roots of his being are in Christ's grave. The oldest oak stands in the grave of the acorn from which it sprang, and to remove it is to destroy it. However massive the tree, it never loses its connection with that buried seed. In the field of wheat, with its millions of blades, every waving stem, with its full grown ear, is rooted in the grave of the kernel of wheat that was buried, that fell into the ground and died that it should not abide alone, but bring forth much fruit. And the whole process of tilling the soil, what is it but making ready the grave by the plough—then burying the seed in the sowing, and then by the harrow filling in the grave?

But the grain of wheat, or the acorn, does not fall into its grave simply to die, but to bring forth fruit, to live anew in the oak or the wheat crop. And we are buried with Christ in order that we may live with him. The literal burial comes after the literal death, and the literal resurrection of the body waits for Christ's coming. But the more important spiritual fact here set forth, is the present participation with Christ in the power of His rising, that even now, we, by the same Spirit, come forth in resurrection power, to walk with Him in newness of life.

This new life by the power of God is to be a new life *unto* God. Hitherto, the life was self-centred, now God-centred. There is a remarkable expression used elsewhere by Paul: for of Him and to Him and through Him are all things (Rom. xi. 36), *i.e.*, God, the source of all, the goal of all, the channel of all. That is the law of the new life—but, of all unrenewed life we must say, of self and to self and through self are all things. Self is the source whence it springs, the great sea into which it finally empties, and the channel through which it flows. The new life will never be unto God, except so far as it is of God; nor will it ever be through God, except so far as it is both of Him and to Him.

Holy living becomes possible to us only in proportion, therefore, as we keep constantly in mind that the power to live a new life of holiness is *wholly of God:* that it is not found in self culture, in education and training, in the most honest purpose or effort, in the most helpful and healthful surroundings, but *solely in an impartation from God*, in the gift of the Spirit of Life, power, holiness, the same that raised up the Lord Jesus; and, that until that Spirit animates and vitalizes us, we are as helpless to live a holy life as Christ's dead body was to move. Not until we realize this can we ever find the power of Christ's Resurrection in ourselves.

And so we must keep as constantly before us

the thought that only as this divinely given life finds its one final object and goal in God, can it find its true direction or develop its true energy. You cannot turn a stream of water whither you will. Water flows freely only in its natural channel. Run it into desert sands and it may be absorbed and sink out of sight. Run it into the midst of a bog and it stagnates in a swamp. Run it among rocks and stones and it winds in and out divided into many streams, perhaps diverted into many channels. The new life, turned into the quicksands of selfish gratification, or the swamp of religious stagnation, or the rocks and stones of a divided and worldly heart, is perverted, sacrificed, lost. But give it God as its one supreme aim and end, and it moves like a mighty and accumulating river. A holy life comes from God, rests in God, and flows through Him as its divine channel. Everything about it is holy—its source, its course, its direction, its end.

There are a few thoughts suggested, most practical and pertinent, such as these:

Our vital connection with Christ is an *endowment* of Power.

Our vital union with Him demands perpetual watchfulness, lest it be hindered or injured. The Endowment is also an *Entrustment.*

1. This vital union with Christ implies and is the Endowment of Power. Holy Living is a supernatural art and cannot be understood by the

natural man, nor enjoyed by the carnal man. We are to think of ourselves as the subjects of miraculous working, as much as when the blind received sight, the deaf, hearing; the lepers, cleansing; the lame, power to walk; or the dead, life. It seems incredible to the unconverted man that, in a moment of time, and simply by turning unto God, and receiving Jesus as a Saviour, he may not only be forgiven, but *enabled to live a new life.* It often seems to him like mockery, because he does not understand that all his previous efforts to live a better life have been the vain struggles of a man without *power*, as though a palsied man should attempt to walk and carry his bed.

Peter's walking on the water illustrates both man's weakness and strength. Our Lord appeared walking the waves of a stormy sea, far enough off for it to seem a ghostly illusion, yet near enough to be heard by those in the boat, perhaps two or three hundred yards away. When he bade Peter " come " unto Him, on the water, the disciple boldly stepped out of the boat and actually walked on the water, and must have gone within arm's length of Jesus, when, beginning to sink, he cried, Lord save, I perish. For Jesus had only to put forth his hand, to catch the sinking man, and they walked back to the boat together. Now observe, while Peter kept his eye on the Lord Jesus, he did just what Jesus did, he walked on the water. But the moment he got his eye off from Him, and thought of the boisterous wind and tossing waves, he lost power and began to sink.

Holy living is as much a miracle to the natural man as is walking on the water, which presents no proper foundation for our feet, having neither stability nor equilibrium, and especially when tossed up and down and driven to and fro by the wind. The secret of Peter's power to triumph over what was otherwise impossible was this, that he was in *touch with Jesus* by faith and had Christ's power in him: and the secret of his sinking is equally plain—he lost touch with Jesus and became as any other impotent mortal, unable to cope with the difficulties of his situation. But what we need now to emphasize is that one moment he was strong to do the impossible, and the next moment utterly weak and sinking. So a human soul can be strong one moment and weak the next, omnipotent or impotent, and it all depends on the touch of faith which brings virtue out of Christ.

An incident in my own pastorate occurs to my mind. A young man, a plumber by trade, came into my house early one morning, to beg my intervention in persuading his wife not to leave him, as she threatened to do, on account of drink. I knew something of her trials, and did not believe such mediation would effect any result; in fact, I doubted whether I ought to attempt to dissuade her from her purpose, for, when drunk, her husband was a brute and her life was sometimes in peril. Even when he sought me, he was but half sober, just recovering from a debauch. I begged him to make separation unnecessary by letting drink alone—but he answered that he could not do it—that he had made trial again and again, succeeding for a few days, but in every case returning again to his cups. He was a church member, but I told him frankly that I felt convinced he knew nothing of the grace and power of God; that the troubles that drive a true child of God to his knees, only drove him to his cups; and I set before him the great truth and fact, that the moment a penitent sinner truly lays hold of Christ, all things are possible to him that believeth.

This Endowment of Life is, however, to be esteemed as a delicate and precious gift to be guarded from injury—an entrustment.

Here we strike one of the most important and awful truths of scripture, generally overlooked. In this chapter we find frequent warnings against continuance in sin, as destructive not only of the power of the new life, but of its existence. And Paul is writing not to, or of, unbelievers; he is addressing Saints. Yet hearken to his words of warning:

"Neither yield ye your members, as instruments of unrighteousness unto sin," and hear his reason: "Know ye not that to whom ye yield yourselves servants to obey, his servants ye are to whom ye obey whether *of sin unto death* or of obedience unto righteousness?" That is—if a disciple yields his members as instruments of unrighteousness, he is yielding to sin, and sin is unto *death*. Again, he says, "the fruit and end of those things is death," and again "the wages of sin is death." Here is a threefold warning addressed to the disciple against going on in sin—sin leads to death, ends in death, and is paid its wages in death. Further on, in chapter viii., he adds that the carnal mind is death.

Life has its laws and conditions, and being the most precious gift of God, must be correspondingly cherished, nourished and guarded. The most precious things are the most susceptible of injury always; worthless weeds it is virtually impossible to exterminate—valuable plants it requires constant care to keep alive. God gives us animal life—it must be fed, and in many ways protected. Food and sleep, air and exercise, rest and recreation are conditions of health. Neglect your animal life for a day and you may fatally harm it. If you have a very rare exotic in your nursery, how you protect it from the ravages of insects, from wintry cold, and from direct violence. Suppose you found some careless boy cutting into its stock with a mischievous hatchet, would you stand by and let such injury go forward?

Every sin tends to death and if persisted in ends in Death as its goal and fruit. What is *death?* It means, in the new Testament, separation from God, loss of fellowship, conscious condemnation and decay of spiritual sensibility. You may have been for years a professing disciple, and have walked with God, but I defy you to commit any deliberate sin against God without at once finding death at work in you. The moment you sin you *fall*, you lose the sense of God's favor, you interrupt your fellowship with Him; you come into conscious condemnation, and you dull and deaden your own sensibilities to the truth and the touch of God.

It is impossible to sin with immunity from spiritual decay and decline, or impunity as to natural penalties.

III

PRACTICAL UNION WITH CHRIST

A WORD may here be said with regard to *Perfection*. Many have a dread of any teaching which, in their judgment, savors of encouraging the notion that sinless perfection is attainable in this world.

1. Let us remember the two senses in which the word *perfect* is used in scripture.

2. Let us remember that even the error of believing one's self perfect is scarcely so bad as the practical error of being contented with habits of sinning.

"Likewise *Reckon* ye also yourselves to be dead indeed unto sin but alive unto God through Jesus Christ our Lord."

Up to this point in the argument we have been occupied with the believer's union with Christ as God has planned and purposed it. We have seen how, in God's eyes and in the scheme of redemption, faith identifies us with the Lord Jesus in death, burial and resurrection; and that the purpose of all this is that we should no longer serve

Sin as a master, but walk in newness of life, living in Christ and with Christ unto God, as those over whom Sin and Death no longer hold mastery.

And now, in one word, Paul turns our thought to the practical aspect of this union with Christ. What does all this mean, and how is this truth to be transmuted into life? How is the believer to reduce this theory to practice? Psalm i. John xv.

The answer begins now to be given, and is found in one word, *Reckon*—the equivalent of another word, *Count*, which occurs first in Genesis, xv. 6. "Abram believed in the Lord and it was counted unto him for righteousness.' Just what he did which was thus counted as righteousness is plain from the exact meaning of the original word—Abram *amened* God. When God said a thing, though it was humanly impossible, Abram said "Amen, it shall be so, even as God hath said." This act of faith, this saying Amen to God is elsewhere described thus: Romans iv. 3, 17–22. See whole passage. Compare with this Hebrews xi. 8–19.

In these passages occur several phrases, all throwing light on the meaning of the word *Reckon*. "Who against hope believed in hope," "considered not his own body now dead when he was about an hundred years old, neither yet the deadness of Sarah's womb." "He staggered not at the promise of God through unbelief, but was strong in faith, giving Glory to God, and being fully persuaded that what he had promised he was able also to perform." Again, in Hebrews, we are told that "Sarah *judged* him faithful who had promised." And again, of Abraham, that in offering up the Son of Promise "he *accounted*," etc., 19. To consider no human impossibilities when God promises; not to stagger in unbelief before the seemingly impassable barriers to blessing, but to be strong in faith, fully persuaded of God's ability and to judge Him faithful, and account Him able even to give back alive what is dead—this is what is meant by Reckoning upon God.

We are told in Rom. iv. 17 that God calleth those things which be not as though they were. This is exactly what faith does in reckoning God faithful. His word has gone forth as to a yet unaccomplished fact; he gives a promise which seems and is, humanly speaking, impossible of fulfilment. Faith, instead of looking at the difficulties, looks at the Promiser; instead of staggering in weakness before the apparent impossibility, the absolute hopelessness of the case, is strong in confidence, giving glory to God in advance of receiving the promise, and, against hope, believes in hope.

Thus, a word that seems to be weak is really strong. To many it is hard to see what difference it makes whether or not I reckon a thing true. If it be true, it is not such reckoning that makes it true, and if it be false, no reckoning can make it other than false. To many so-called believers, to reckon or count is simply to *imagine*, and implies only credulity, amusing one's self with one's own fancies.

Such entirely miss the true thought that lies behind the word reckon. So far is it from being a mere vain imagination to reckon on God's word as an accomplished fact, that it is the *soul and substance of faith:*

Seven blessed results may be traced to such *reckoning* of faith.

1. First of all it is a tribute of faith to God's ability, willingness, love and faithfulness.
2. It is a challenge of faith, indirectly moving God to show himself the faithful Promiser.
3. It is an attitude of faith, waiting in expectation of blessing.
4. It is, therefore, a removal of the limits which unbelief places upon God.
5. It is an opening of the heart to the full reception of promised good.
6. It is the basis of all active obedience and hearty self-surrender.
7. It is the secret of a peaceful, hopeful, courageous triumph over foes, etc.

Reckoning is, therefore, a form of faith. It counts Him faithful who promised. To a true believer God's word is God's work; His promise is His performance. With man a word and even an oath may utterly fail, but God is unchangeable.

He speaks and it is done—it stands fast. Hence, in prophecy, we find the tenses of the verb used indiscriminately, an event that lies a thousand years ahead being spoken of as *present* or even *past*. Comp. Isaiah liii. The Word of God was so accepted and counted on as certain to be accomplished, that the language of prophecy predicting coming events is the language of history recording past events.

It is easy to see that such reckoning on God's faithfulness is the highest possible honor that can be placed on His word. Indeed, without such faith it is impossible to please Him—Heb. xi. 6.

In Hebrews iii. occurs that remarkable phrase *The* provocation. Notice the definite article as though *one* form of offence was selected out of all the actual and possible sins against God, as the one unbearable sin. What was it? simply *unbelief* which does not reckon on God. In the desert wanderings for forty years God's people constantly provoked God in this way. He told them that He brought them out that He might bring them in. Deut. vi. 23. And referred them constantly to his miracles of interposition in their behalf in Egypt as proof and example of His power and grace, and the pledge of what He both could and would do for them in the actual possessing of the Land of Promise. But they believed not His words, they feared the giant Anakim, they murmured against God and many a time they threatened to go back into Egypt. Thus their unbelief was a four-fold provocation : first it was an assault on God's truth and made Him a liar; upon His power, for it counted Him as weak and unable to bring them in; upon His immutability, for, although they did not say so, their course implied that He was a changeable God, and could not *do* the wonders He had once wrought. And unbelief was also an assault upon His fatherly faithfulness, as though He would encourage an expectation He had no intention of fulfilling. On the contrary, Caleb and Joshua honored God by accounting His word absolutely true, His power infinite, His disposition unchangingly gracious, and His faithfulness such that He would never awaken any hope which He would not bring to fruition.

There are two conspicuous instances in which our Lord said "great is thy faith. I have not found so great faith; no, not in Israel:" the instance of the Centurion, Matt. viii., and of the woman of Canaan, Matt. xv. In both cases the greatness of the faith consisted in this one thing : they reckoned upon God. The Centurion besought Christ in behalf of his servant, sick of palsy. And when Jesus said, "I will come and heal him," he replied, "I am not worthy that Thou shouldst come under my roof. *Speak the word only* and my servant shall be healed." For the first and only time in His public ministry, He found a man who, instead of insisting on some visible sign and wonder—a personal visit of the Master—*preferred* to rest simply on Christ's spoken word. And the woman of Canaan is still more remarkable in that, having no encouraging word of promise on which to lean, herself an outcast Canaanite, met at first with silence and then with apparent refusal and even personal rebuff, she counted on Christ's power and grace so confidently, in the absence of all encouragements to faith, that she would not be sent away without the blessing, actually turning repulse into an argument in her favor. "Go thy way, the devil is gone out of thy daughter." The study of the history of Christ's personal life among men, and, in fact, of the entire history of God's people, shows that to take God at His word and count every promise as true, resting upon it as if it were already fulfilled, is of the very essence of faith.

When the nobleman of Capernaum sought healing for his son, who was at the point of death, Christ said, "Go thy way, thy son liveth," and the man believed, went his way, and so counted on the word of Christ that he did not go home *that day;* but, although Cana and Capernaum were not ten miles apart, he seems to have stopped on the way till the next day. And the great lesson of that narrative is, whatsoever He saith unto you *trust* it.

When the ten lepers sought healing (Luke xvii.) Christ bade them go show themselves to the priest as if already whole—to be pronounced clean, and released from ceremonial and social restraints and restrictions. And *as they went* they were cleansed —*i.e.*, because they counted on the word of Christ, and proceeded as though already the blessing was theirs—they had what they sought.

If the greatness of faith then lay in this, that God was reckoned on as true, faithful, loving, gracious, and changeless, in all these, the littleness of faith and the greatness of unbelief must lie in the opposite course—God is *not counted* on; practically His word is treated as a lie, or as untrustworthy. The actual *work*, the wonder wrought, must be seen, for only seeing is believing.

While, therefore, Faith makes mighty works possible, men limit God by unbelief, so that He cannot do mighty works. Comp. Psalm lxxviii., cvi. While faith opens the door of the heart to a promised blessing, unbelief closes it, and so shuts out God's gift and God's presence.

It is not too much to say, therefore, that to reckon on God is the soul of faith and the basis of all fellowship with Him. Christ could not do many mighty works in Nazareth because of the unbelief of His fellow-townsmen, who, remembering Him as the carpenter's son, counted Him unable to teach or work with divine power. Again, let it be said, so far as I reckon God able and willing, true and faithful, and that every word He has spoken He can and will fulfil, I make possible, both for Him to impart and for myself to receive the blessing He yearns to bestow. Hence the immense, intense significance of that oft-recurring phrase, "According to your faith be it unto you." Every measure of blessing is determined by the measure of faith.

We can see something quite analogous to this in our relations with our fellowmen. Harmonious and happy relations are impossible without a basis of faith. Take the credit system—the word *credit* is from *credo*, I believe. You sell goods to a customer, counting on his ability and fidelity in paying his bills ; and the whole banking system is simply counting on others' trustworthiness. What is a promissory note but a note that is a promise? You have actually nothing but a piece of paper as to actual value—worthless—but you count on the solvency and honesty of the man whose signature is on it—that he has means and will to pay it, and you use that worthless piece of paper as currency ; it passes from hand to hand as though it were gold.

"If thou canst *believe*," said Christ to him who said, "If *Thou* canst *do* anything," etc.

The link between the faith that reckons God's word true and the actual reception of blessing is a link that *in the nature of things* exists. To count on God's word brings *peace*. Here is a lad that says to his father, "When you come home tonight bring me a penknife," and his father says, "I will." Careful not to promise a child what he does not mean to do, and careful to do all he has promised, he buys the knife and comes home with it in his pocket. And when at night he meets his boy, the child does not say, "Well, I suppose you have not brought me the knife you promised," etc., but simply comes up, puts his hand in his father's pocket and takes out the knife. God likes to have us confide likewise in our Father's word, and without a doubt come and lay hold of the promised blessing. This is the secret of all peace.

Mr. George Müller has been observed by his helpers to be quite as serene and joyful in God when there is not a shilling in the bank or a loaf of bread in the larder, wherewith to cloth and feed his 2,000 orphans as when there is a plenty, both of money and of food. And the only explanation of such a phenomenon which has confronted an unbelieving world and half believing church for a half-century, says one of those same helpers of this patriarch of Bristol, is that maxim of Mr. Müller himself, that "where anxiety begins Faith ends, and where faith begins anxiety ends." For him to count on God is to dismiss all care. If he has no money in the bank, God's riches are inexhaustible; and if he has no food in the larder, his God has infinite supplies for all his need, and there shall be no lack.

We are especially concerned now with the bearing of this matter upon holiness—in its two great aspects: abandonment of known sin and obedience to known duty. Elsewhere in this epistle Paul says, "Put ye on the Lord Jesus Christ, and *make not provision for the flesh* to fulfil the lusts thereof." —Rom. xiii. 14. All our life long we are making provision, either for certainties or for uncertainties. Some things we know we shall need, such as food and raiment, a home and the like necessities; other things we may need as crises arise, such as sickness, loss of property, bereavement, etc. To-day we have made provision for immediate wants. As we expect to live, we provide for the night's lodging and to-morrow's meals. Now, if you knew that to-night, at midnight, death would certainly end your mortal career, you would at once stop making provision for living. A shroud, a coffin, a grave, would be all the clothing, house, possession, you would need. God would have you count yourself dead to sin and hence living no longer therein, and reckon yourself alive unto God and unto holiness.

Your expectation has everything to do with your actual life. If you expect to sin you will sin, and if you expect not to sin, because you reckon yourself no longer under sin's mastery, but under God's, you will find that expectation itself a security. Paul says we are saved by hope, and, in the armor of God, the very helmet is the hope of salvation. To count on sinning is itself a form of sinning; it is reckoning the flesh, the world, the Devil, mightier than the Spirit of God and the Son of God, whose very office it is to overcome the flesh, deliver us from this present evil age, and destroy the works of the Devil. A veteran of Waterloo used to tell how the trained soldiers of Wellington, the night before that decisive battle that turned the destinies of Europe, took the raw recruits and told them of the skill, the capacity, the courage of their great commander and so inspired them with confidence in the Iron Duke, that, however the battle might seem to waver, the ultimate issue might be confidently expected to be victory and so those raw recruits went into battle expecting victory and reckoning defeat impossible.*

When Christ told the blind man, whose eyes he anointed with clay, to go to the pool of Siloam and wash, he may have had someone to guide him to the pool, but if he counted the Lord's word as faithful, he dismissed him there, even before he washed. The unbelieving man, even when he outwardly submits to God's command, timidly experiments on God. He holds fast his earthly guides and helpers—lest the Lord fail him. If he goes to the pool at all he says to his guide: "If the Lord's word is true in my case and I receive my sight, I shall not need you on the way back. Wait and see whether I receive my sight." The true believer dismisses his guide at the pool—even before he applies the waters to his eyes. Has not his Lord

* See Asa Mahan's "Out of Darkness into Light."

spoken? He counts on seeing, and in advance casts away all other dependence. That faith not only honors God, it is a challenge to him to honor his own word. It constrains and compels him to be faithful, if he were in need of any such constraint or compulsion. The very fact that his humble follower leans on him, trusts in him, reckons upon him, makes it, if possible, the more certain of his interposition. When Abraham had prayed for Sodom, with, do doubt, an especial thought for Lot's family, God remembered Abraham, though he did not spare the city, and brought out Lot; and hear him say, as he hastened the tardy steps of Lot:—" Haste thee, for I cannot do anything till thou be come thither!" As though He was hindered in an act of righteous judgment by the yet unsafe position of the man for whom Abraham had besought him.

IV

ACTUAL UNION WITH CHRIST

"Let not sin, therefore, reign in your mortal body, that ye should obey it in the lusts thereof—

"Neither yield ye your members, as instruments of unrighteousness unto sin;

"But yield yourselves unto God as those that are alive from the dead; and your members as instruments of righteousness unto God;

"For sin shall not have dominion over you,

"For ye are not under the law but under grace."
—Verses 12 to 23.

Here we touch the point in this great argument where the believer's union with Christ actually affects his daily life, and effects the one grand result, definite holy living. This is a distinct advance on any previous step or stage of the argument. We reach here the supreme point of *application*. The judicial union shows us how God construes our relation to Christ as one with him before the Law; the vital presents that oneness as implying also a sharing of His Life, and its Spirit of power; the practical union teaches how we are to construe our union with Him as to the confidence it inspires. And, now, all that has been said reaches its grand application: what is to be the *actual effect* on my life? If the whole passage be carefully examined it will be found again that at least seven answers are given, for in every part of this argument we find a complete seven-foldness, which strangely marks it and stamps it.

As in the previous section the great word was RECKON, in this, the great word is YIELD.

First, Negative—Yield not allegiance to sin, the old master. Yield not your members as instruments of sin.

Second, Positive—Yield yourself and your members unto God. Yield *in faith*, to the enablement of Grace. Yield by *practical surrender* to Christ as Master. Yield by *receiving* from the heart his teaching.

And so claim, possess, enjoy, the full gift of eternal life.

It is also plain and emphatic that the true way not to yield to sin is to yield unto God. Man would naturally say: Let not sin, therefore, reign in your mortal body, neither yield ye your members unto sin; but *resist* sin, and *fight* desperately at every point. But the Spirit says not so: the most successful fight against Sin and Satan is the actual surrender of faith and obedience to the new Master. The soul is never strong in the attitude of simple resistance. Overcome evil *with good.* Occupy yourself with God, and displace evil by good. This is the idea of Chalmers in his " Expulsive Power of a New Affection."

1. I am to disown henceforth all allegiance to sin as my master.
2. To withhold my members from all service of sin as his instruments.
3. To yield myself unto God and my members as instruments.
4. To trust myself to the enabling power of Grace.
5. To accept Christ as my Master and practically obey him.
6. To receive from the heart the mould of God's teaching.
7. To claim and enjoy in all its fulness the gift of Eternal Life.

At every step here it is plain that actual victory over sin is contemplated, and positive holiness, exhibited in character and conduct. I am to think of myself as God thinks of me, and make the judicial and vital union with Christ a reality, by practically counting upon God's power and love, and actually exchanging the Sovereignty of sin for the Mastership of Christ.

This point in the argument can best be understood by the change from *standing* to *state.* Standing represents our judicial position before God, condemnation exchanged for justification, and alienation for reconciliation. God counts us no longer sinners and enemies, but gives us a new standing as sons and heirs. Our state must correspond with our standing. Being sons we must exhibit His image and likeness; being heirs, we must be prepared for our inheritance. We saw that a judicial acquittal implies no necessary actual change in character: it is simply an act of sovereign mercy and grace — a declarative act. But God cannot compromise with sin or tolerate evil in us, and justification would be a bargain with evil doing if it did not contemplate and eventuate in sanctification as an actual *state*. God never, therefore, justifies without sanctifying. He first counts or reckons us holy in Christ and then proceeds to make us holy, until at last we are presented before the presence of His glory, without rebuke, or spot, or wrinkle, blame or blemish, unrebukable and perfect. We must remember, therefore, the calling of sons and the destiny of heirs and keep before us that great injunction and invitation: "Be ye Holy, for I am holy."

Let not sin therefore reign; this implies both a *privilege* and a *power* to resist the further sovereignty of sin. Do not longer *allow* sin to rule over you; this would be a mockery of my helplessness if I am impotent to resist.

Sin is here impersonated as a tyrannical master, once obeyed and served, but whose reign is now at an end and his power broken.

How am I to meet his demands and maintain my position of resistance? That is the first practical question.

The answer is: By my *Identification* with Christ.

We have seen how the whole life of Christ as the Last Adam was representative, and how every great crisis in that life has its encouraging lesson for us. Let us consider His *Temptation* in its bearing on this subject. Forty days at the beginning of Christ's public life strangely correspond with another forty days at its close. One represents the complete victory over the *Devil* and the other the glorious conquest over *death*. Why was Christ tempted? not, surely, for His own sake, but that, having suffered being tempted, he might be able to succor them that are now tempted; so that every tempted soul may now come boldly unto the Throne of Grace, knowing that we have a great High Priest, who knows our infirmities, and has compassion on the ignorant and them that are out of the way, etc.

To compare Adam's Temptation with Christ's will show that they were strangely identical. Each was an appeal to the lust of the flesh, the lust of the eyes and the Pride of life. And it is plain that our Lord met the Tempter, not on His own account, but as our representative, the Last Adam. Therefore, everything about that experience has a significance for us: the methods of Satanic approach, the methods of Messianic resistance, and the final complete victorious issue, are all on record for our learning and encouragement.

For example, we learn how subtle are Satan's wiles. He suggested to Christ unlawful ways of gratifying and satisfying natural and sinless cravings. Having no sinful propensities to appeal to, in the perfect man, he addressed such innocent desires as hunger, and the yearning for self-vindication, for the speedy accomplishment of his mission, etc. But the *ways* he suggested to attain these lawful ends would have compromised faith, dependence on God and self-surrender; they would have exhibited a lack of confidence in God's Fatherhood and Providence, or presumption in an unwarranted exposure to danger, or an attempt to fight God's war with the Devil's weapons. Whatever the exact character of Christ's temptation, it is enough to know that He was tempted in all points like as we are, yet without sin, and that, having suffered being tempted, He is able to succor them that are tempted.

It is particularly to be noticed that He successfully resisted the Devil and finally actually repulsed him by the simple use of the Word of God. His sole attitude was resistance: He stood firm, and never came into close quarters with the Tempter as in a deadly grapple or violent wrestle. He calmly stood like a man with folded arms who fearlessly looks a foe in the face and defies him;

and the only weapon He used was a text of Scripture—the sword of the Spirit which He thrust at Satan, and by which He at last drove him back. Moreover, Christ's conquest was representative. In His victory every believer is a victor, and for him also, so far as he is in Christ, Satan is a vanquished foe. He knows that no temptation ever befalls him but such as is common to man, such as for him Christ underwent, such as, in Christ, saints of all ages have met and resisted. The believer is to meet Satan, therefore, as Christ did—folding his arms, take his stand, look him in the face, defy him, and answer all his subtleties with a word of Scripture. He is to be perfectly assured in advance that Satan's power is forever broken. One of the Spirit's convictions wrought in men is that the Prince of this World *is* judged, not is to *be* judged, but is already judged. Christ met him, defeated him, drove him back, put him to rout, and Satan *knows* that his sceptre is wrested from his grasp by a mightier than he and his empire shattered. He will boast and seek to intimidate us by his threats, but we are to understand that his power over us is only so far as we *concede him control*. We may allow ourselves to be taken captive of him at his will, and so fall into his snare; but if we put on the whole armor of God and simply *stand*, we shall withstand in the evil day and, having done all, still stand unmoved, using only the same sword of the Spirit as Christ used.

This we emphasize because of a common notion, most misleading and unscriptural, that Satan is practically omnipotent, and that, like some giant, he holds and carries us as helpless babes—that, like some resistless lion, he prowls about seeking whom he may devour, and if we come into contact with him he will tear us in pieces and there will be none to deliver; or, again, men talk of tidal-waves of temptation that sweep them off their feet and carry them whither they will. All this is, I believe, a devil's lie, invented to put us more helplessly at Satan's mercy.

It is a remarkable fact that, in three cases of New Testament reference to Satan, beside the two accounts of our Lord's temptation, we are distinctly taught that all we have to do is to *stand*. James, who has so much to say about temptation, writes, "Submit yourselves to God: Resist the Devil and he will flee from you," iv. 7.

Notice this language: *Resist* and he will *flee*. How does this comport with current notions about Satan's irresistible power over men. Can a weak and puny babe resist a giant, and drive him back by simple resistance? If you resist a tidal-wave, will it flee? will it not rather be you that flee?

Turn now to the testimony of Peter: "Be sober, be vigilant, because your adversary, the Devil, as a roaring lion walketh about seeking whom he may devour: whom resist, stedfast in the faith, knowing that the same afflictions are accomplished in your brethren that are in the world" (1 Peter v. 8, 9). Here the Devil is represented as a lion, prowling about, roaring, and looking for his prey; but so far from hinting that any saint is absolutely at his mercy, how positive is the teaching that all we have to do is to keep watchful, maintain a holy sobriety, and take the attitude of resistance. We are to keep vigilant lest we be taken unawares in subtle snares; we are to keep sober, lest we lose power to stand firm and maintain the attitude of resistance; but here again we are plainly taught that Satan can do nothing with a child of God who watches his movements, keeps prayerful, and stands firm and strong in Christ. And we are encouraged to remember that other tempted saints are daily meeting and, by the same grace, resisting this great adversary. If such scriptures teach anything, it is that Satan has no power over us against our will to compel us to sin. He can do nothing with us except as we concede to him power over us.

The apostle John is no less explicit. In a part of his first epistle, which is given to the warning against the power of evil spirits, and especially the arch enemy of God and man, he uses language as remarkable as any in the New Testament (1 John iv. 4). Here the victory is represented as an accomplished fact, and every disciple is taught that in himself there dwells One who is greater than all these evil spirits that are in the world. The saint is a fortress, held and commanded by the Divine Spirit, and no enemy can prevail against Him. "Ye are of God little children and have overcome them—the spirits of evil; because greater is He that is in you than he that is in the world."

There is one passage in Paul's writings which at first seems to give color to the idea that in defeating Satan we must at least consent to a deadly hand-to-hand grapple (Ephesians vi. 10-16). Here we are told that our wrestling is not against flesh and blood only, but against the whole hierarchy of fallen angels. But let us read further and see how we are to meet these foes. "Strong in the Lord and in the power of His might, we have only to withstand"—notice the repetition of this word—"that ye may be able to stand against the wiles of the devil, able to withstand in the evil day, having done all to stand." And so he concludes: "*Stand therefore.*" God has provided an armor of resistance, covering the disciple from head to foot; and clothed in that panoply he cannot be overcome. When Satan hurls his most terrible weapons, his fiery darts, the shield of faith needs only to be held up to receive them, and they are quenched, and the one and only offensive weapon represented as to be employed is the sword of the Spirit, which is the word of God.

I am, therefore, *not to yield* to Satan, but calmly,

resolutely, to resist and dispute at every point his claims and advances.

But in the word of God we are never left to the *negative;* the positive is always added. We are to withhold our tongues from filthiness and foolish talking and jesting, and use them for ministering grace to the hearer. We are to put off all that ill becomes a child of God, but put on whatsoever is holy and beautiful in temper and conduct.

Let us look now at the positive teaching of the word. We are not to be content with *resistance;* there is a positive *persistence*—a persevering endeavor, a running a race, etc.

"Present your bodies a living sacrifice. Be not conformed, but be ye transformed" (Rom. xii.). The only hope of *not* being conformed to this world is that I am transformed. I shall vainly seek not to yield to Satan if I do not actually yield to God. I must *have a service* of some sort to employ me, and if it be not God's it will be the Devil's. If no man can serve two masters, neither can any man serve none. *Idleness is* service to the Devil. The only way to know that I am strong is to use my strength; the use of it both makes one conscious of it and increases it.

This lesson is taught here and elsewhere so beautifully that we may well stop to learn it. Let us look at it, first, in its relations to obedience to God; second, as to soundness of doctrine, and third, as to consistency of life.

Here we meet a very emphatic command: "Yield yourselves unto God, and your members as instruments of righteousness unto God. For sin shall not have dominion over you; for ye are not under the law, but under grace."

Here is a command, a motive, an encouragement. We are not under law, but under grace. Law enjoins, but does not enable. It puts before us a standard, but gives no power to obey and overcome. Grace still puts before us a high and holy standard, abating not a jot or tittle of the high claims of obedience, but it adds gracious energy, strength, enabling power. To that enabling power we are to entrust ourselves to do and bear the whole will of God. We are to accept this grace as the guaranty for obedience and conformity to God. And while it makes us strong to resist Satan and sin, it is to make us equally strong to receive and obey the known will of God. Our body is the temple of God. Let Him occupy and consecrate His own Temple, and let every part of it be sacredly given up to his inhabitation.

Again, the Apostle teaches us to yield ourselves to God's holy teaching (v. 17). God be thanked that ye who *were* the slaves of sin, have received from the heart that mould of teaching whereunto ye were delivered. The figure seems to be that of a matrix or mould, such as is used to give plastic clay or wax, or molten metal, a desired shape. God has a definite mould of teaching, and so has the Devil, and we are carefully to distinguish between them, and beware to *what sort of doctrine* we submit ourselves. God's great matrix of character is *His word*. If we get thoroughly acquainted with *that*, and fully yield ourselves to its influence, we shall take on its whole impression until we grow to be scriptural believers. That word is to be the final arbiter in every controversy: To the law and to the Testimony. One of the subtlest devices of the devil is to offer us a type of teaching that is plausible and pleasing to the natural heart, and recommends itself by the fact that many professed believers accept it—nay, it is even outwardly and in some things conformed to the word of God, but is really unscriptural in its essence; it leaves out, if it does not contradict—vital truths.

Dr. A. J. Gordon used to say that a certain popular preacher was a first-class preacher of the secondary truths of our holy faith, but that his preaching entirely lacked the primary truths, such as atonement by blood, Regeneration by the Spirit, etc.

If you submit yourself to unscriptural teaching, however recommended by illustrious names, you will take its impress and begin to doubt the verities of religion. One of the marks by which you may know Satan's mould of doctrine is that it leaves *doubt* instead of *faith*. He leads men to think the Gospel mould is *narrow* and *cramped*, that it may do for women and children and small men, for ignorance, superstition and credulity, but not for the intelligent and wise and great. And so people, who once believed, learn to doubt their beliefs and believe their doubts, if they do not go further and hold beliefs positively opposed to the divine teaching.

Now, the one rule for a disciple is to devoutly study his Bible and yield himself to its teaching. In other departments men *know* in order to *believe;* in God's school we must *believe* and *obey* in order fully to *know,* for it is only as we practically test this mould of teaching by conformity to it, that we actually learn its perfection. But to all who thus test it, by daily conformity and prayerful obedience, it becomes supremely satisfactory. One becomes more and more eager to know what it teaches and obey all its commands. Obedience is found to be delight and the organ of clearer vision. God's word is found and eaten and, like food, gives both joy and strength.

In the epistle to the Colossians Paul very beautifully shows us how much the consistency and beauty of a Godly life depends on this perpetual and prayerful subjection to God.—Chap. iii. The epistle is a sort of commentary on these three chapters in Romans. In the first two chapters the union of the Believer with Christ is presented in its judicial and vital aspects; and then, at the third chapter, the practical and actual begin to be put before us: "If ye then *be risen* with Christ," etc.

Note the following injunctions, all based upon the fact that we are one with Christ in death and resurrection life:

1. Seek those things which are above; *i.e.*, look up to your risen Lord.
2. Set your affection on things above; *i.e.*, mount up and look down on earth from heaven.
3. Mortify therefore your members which are upon the earth; *i.e.*, live there and let what is down here *die*.
4. Put off all these:
5. Put on therefore: above all these things put on charity.
6. Even as Christ forgave you, so also do ye.
7. Let the peace of God rule.
8. Be ye thankful.
9. Let the word of Christ dwell richly in you.
10. Whatsoever ye do, do all in the name of the Lord Jesus.

Here we have ten general exhortations, all based on the argument in chapters i. and ii.

Upon two of these exhortations we may fix our thought: "*Put off.*" "*Put on.*"

At first we meet a seeming paradox: Paul says ye *have* put *off* the old man and yet he says *put off* all these; and again ye *have* put *on* the new man, and yet adds *put on*, etc., and, stranger still, he makes the fact that we have put off and put on the *reason* for putting off and putting on. But now ye also put off all these, *seeing that* ye have put off; ye have put on, therefore put on. How shall we reconcile these contradictions?

1. We must make *actually true* what is *judicially true* and let our state correspond with our standing. Ye have died judicially, mortify therefore your members—*be dead* actually. Judicially ye have put off the old man and put on the new man, now practically and actually put off and put on.

2. But it is, perhaps, a fuller and clearer explanation to note *just what* we are said to have put off and put on, and what we are bidden to put off and put on. Ye have put off the *old man*, now put off all these also which belong to the old man; ye have put on the new man, now put on all that belongs to the new man. Life must be consistent to be complete and beautiful. When Christ rose and came out of the sepulchre he could not leave corruption behind, for his flesh never saw corruption. From his birth that "holy thing," born of the virgin, was immaculate and, with no taint of sin, could not decay. Hence, even the body of Christ is called in Psalm xvi., Thy Holy One—incapable of corruption. But Christ did leave behind the only thing that savored of corruption — his grave clothes, and this is particularly noted in the Gospel according to John. Comp. xix. 40, xx. 5-7. The narrative is very specific. John himself saw the linen clothes lying there, and both he and Peter,

on closer examination, saw the linen clothes that wrapped his body lying in the sepulchre, and the cloth that wrapped his head, not lying with the rest, but in a separate place. When our Lord arose and came out of the tomb, he had no further use for grave clothes, and they were conspicuously left behind. They would have been both unbecoming and cumbersome to a risen and active Redeemer; and as they belonged to death and the grave, they were *all*, even the cloth that wrapped his thorn-crowned head, all deposited and left behind in the place of death. And yet Christ went not forth naked. Whence came those resurrection robes we know not, but they were not the same as he wore before crucifixion, for those had been parted among the mocking soldiers.

How clear the lesson. Have you been buried with Christ? leave in his grave all that belongs to the old man, for all this belongs to death and corruption. Have you risen with Christ? put on all the garments of glory and beauty that belong to the new man. You were clad in pride, be clothed with humility; you were invested in your own righteousness, which you see to be filthy rags; now put on Christ, and in Him the righteousness of God.

The grave clothes that belonged to the old man have about them the association and infection of sin, the contagion of Evil. Hence Jude bids us, even when pulling sinners out of the fire, to hate even the garment spotted by the flesh. I heard, from a friend, of a most malignant case of disease in which, after the death of certain victims, everything which had been associated with the disease was ordered to be burned; subsequently the same disease attacked another member of the family, and was due to the preservation, from the fire, of a beautiful sofa cushion which had been used as a pillow by those who had first fallen a prey to the destroyer. Whatever is associated with a life of sin should be cast off and renounced, if we are to be safe from the infection and contagion of this soul-destroying disease. Every garment spotted by the flesh is to be hated.

A friend in Newport told me of his early history and how he was enabled to meet and defeat every temptation by a simple resort to scripture. When tempted to marry an ungodly woman, because of personal attractions and wealth, he read in the word, "only in the Lord." When tempted to crowd out a neighboring tradesman, whose premises he wanted to add to his own, he read "devise not mischief by thy neighbor, seeing he dwelleth securely by thee," etc. In every crisis of temptation a word of scripture sufficed.

But let the Word of God further instruct us. We are told *what* to put off and put on. *Put off* all these: Anger, wrath, malice, blasphemy, filthy communication out of your mouth; lie not one to another.

Put on bowels of mercies, kindness, humbleness of mind, meekness, long suffering, forbearing and forgiving one another, and above or outside all these, put on Charity, which is the bond of perfectness. To the old, unrenewed, carnal man, anger, wrath and malice—sins of temper—blasphemy and filthy talking and lying—sins of tongue—were natural and befitting corruption. To the new man, renewed in knowledge and image of God, mercy, kindness and humility, meekness, long suffering and forgiveness are the only appropriate belongings; and the very girdle that, outside of all these, binds them together and keeps them in place is that Love that is the bond of perfectness.

V

MARITAL UNION WITH CHRIST

HERE we may well take shoes off our feet as on holy ground. The next aspect of the believer's union with Jesus Christ is taken from *Marriage*, and hence is called *Marital*. Here it is the figure of a second marriage, the obligation and relation involved in the former being dissolved by death, so that the woman, thus left free by the decease of her husband, marries another man.

"Know ye not how that the law hath dominion over a man as long as *he liveth?* etc.

"Wherefore ye also are become dead to the law by the body of Christ that ye should be married to another, even to him who is raised from the dead, that we should bring forth fruit unto God." That, and the following verse constitute the key of this part of the argument.

One difficulty confronts us—what seems a hopeless mixture of figures. In the first part of the representation it is the party that is under the dominion of the law which is personified as husband, that is supposed to live, while the husband dies; but in the latter it is the party married to the law that becomes dead to the law, so that for a consistent figure it must now be the law that survives and enters into a second union.

We may solve the difficulty by saying, as is often done, that no figure is adequate to represent such truth, and so, dismissing it as an *analogy*, accept it simply as a *parable*, applicable at a single point of resemblance. If we adopt such method of interpretation, it is plain that the vital matter is this: a previous and binding relation is somehow dissolved, released by death, and the surviving party is free to enter into a new relation. As a matter of fact the believing penitent sinner has in Christ found such release from a previous legal relation and has become Christ's own bride.

But there is a deeper solution, for we are touching a deeper mystery. Christ died, but it was not possible that he should be holden of death; hence He who died also lives forevermore. And so the believer who in Him died also in Him lives. Both things are, therefore, true. In one aspect of the believer's experience he is dead, and so cannot enter into any new union; in another he lives from the dead and is, therefore, open to a new marital relation. In a sense it is the law that survives, while the sinner dies under its penalty. In another sense it is the law that dies as a rule of Justification and as a controlling and Condemning Power over the sinner, while the sinner lives as a believer, to be free to be married unto Him on whom all his desire is now centred.

We begin now to see why Paul refers to that first marriage in Eden as a Mystery concerning Christ and the Church. Adam slept, and during his sleep God took a rib from his side and from it made woman, and the woman became wife. Adam's sleep was the type and prophecy of Christ's death, which is at once the death of the sinner and the birth of the believer. Adam's re-awaking was the type and prophecy of Christ's resurrection, making possible the wedlock of the believer with his Lord.

In this figure of husband and wife we touch the most complete and wonderful figure, thus far found in scripture, to present the union of the believer with Christ. And it is found in the Old and New Testaments alike, perhaps the one ideal that most pervades the scripture. It meets us first, in Genesis, in the typical wedlock of Adam and Eve, and last, in the Revelation, in the marriage of the Lamb and his bride. Most wonderful, perhaps, is the fact that the controlling conception is that of a marriage with one who has been the wife —nay the cast-off, adulterous wife of another. Nothing is more moving and melting in point of pathos of love, the poetry of tenderness, than some of these Old Testament portrayals of Redeeming Grace. For example, Ezekiel xvi., where we reach the lowest point in the degradation of the adulterous woman, and the highest point of grace in her restoration and reconciliation.

The great central point whence we must survey the marriage relation as the chosen symbol and parable of the Believer's union with Christ is this—the IDENTITY OF LIFE FOUNDED UPON LOVE. It will be seen that we have constantly been mounting higher and higher in the study of this great argument. In the Judicial union it was the identity of the last Adam with those whom he represented as Head of a Race; in the vital union it was the identity of the Lord of Life with those whom, by His Spirit, He quickens. In the practical union, it was the identity of a Leader and Champion with those who follow him; and in the actual union it was the Identity of a Sovereign and Master with those who yield to Him in holy subjection. But now it is the identity of Husband with the Wife who is to him bone of his bone, flesh of his flesh. Partnership indeed, but the highest of which we know.

Let us stop to notice the closeness of this unity and the perfection of this identity.

The wife loses herself and her separate entity and identity in her husband. Originally drawn from his side she was called woman, because taken out of man; and in marriage she is counted as in a sense returning to her place within him, nearest his heart, to be again part of his very personality.

Hence she leaves even father and mother to cleave unto him; she gives up her family name and takes his; forsakes her family home to make her home with him; her property and even herself she surrenders to his control, and even her own will and way become henceforth subordinate—no longer twain, but one flesh. And a greater mystery is the result of this—for the two lives thus made one, become the united source of life; marriage is the secret of parentage, and through it Adam begat a son in his own likeness, another type of the holy fruitfulness of true believers.

What shall we say, then, of the exceeding riches of the unsearchable grace here presented to our thought? We can only stand in awe before such a truth and look up as before a mountain whose top is lost in clouds, as to something that is high, so that we cannot attain unto it. That the great God in Christ should stoop so low and lift us so high, that he should actually take us out of the filth of our lusts and raise us to the dignity of a bride that shares the ecstasy and purity of holy love! This is incredible but for the fact that He himself so declares it to be.

And if you are ever tempted to bring down the word of God to a human level, and doubt its inspiration, turn to the fifth chapter of Ephesians and ask yourself what but a divinely taught pen could ever have represented the wife as exalted to so sublime a plane. Read the seven-fold descrip-

tion of Christ's Husbandly Devotion to His own Church :
He *loved* her and *gave Himself* for her.
He *sanctified* her and *cleansed* her.
He *nourishes* and *cherishes* her.
He *will present her* to himself.

Now this marvellous picture of the Divine Husband's lavish love for his believing Bride is professedly drawn from marriage, and yet earthly wedlock at its best furnished no model for such a picture. In Paul's day there was not a husband on earth who thus thought of or treated his wife, even among the chosen nation, God's peculiar people, or even where there was true love and tender attachment. What husband ever so lost himself in his wife as to sacrifice himself for her, loving her not for her purity and innocence, but despite her impurity and guilt; instead of being dependent for his love upon her virtuous loyalty, consecrating himself to her sanctification and cleansing, overcoming her weakness and alienation by a nourishing care and a cherishing tenderness, and finally presenting her to himself, made all that she is by his own unselfish transforming Love? Most marital love is a love of complacence, answering to the attraction of beautiful character; here it is a love of benevolence, bestowed notwithstanding the repulsion of wickedness and abomination, and persistently holding on until perfection takes the place of deformity and depravity. Tell us, ye who count the Bible a human book, whence Paul drew his artist's model for this fairest portrait of wedlock to be found in all literature? Could he have penned this description had he not been taught of God?

This relation is one of the highest power and privilege, and hence it is here presented in its bearing on our noncontinuance in sin.

Marriage is the sphere of *blessing:* 1, identity. 2, blessed possession, etc. If the wife surrenders herself, she meets in a high sense a surrender of Love to herself; she gives, and in giving gets. She says "I am his," but she can add "my beloved is mine." It is a mutual *possession.* So the believer can say in Christ, My Lord and My God.

Marriage is the sphere of *privilege.* It brings the wife into the intimacies of her husband's life. There is a sharing of thoughts and love and purpose, so that in a true wedlock there comes to be a unity found nowhere else. Discord there cannot be, because two hearts with all their desires and hopes are made one. So of Christ and the believer.

Marriage is the sphere of *parentage.* Eve was the mother of all the living, because Adam was the father of all the living and she was his wife. "Be fruitful and multiply and replenish the earth and subdue it," was the command God addressed to the first wedded pair. Dominion over the lower sphere of nature depended on multiplication of the higher orders of life, and only so can be understood the typical force of that formal and ideal marriage which forecast the wedlock between Christ and His church. Mary the Virgin could become the mother of the Messiah only as the power of the Highest overshadowed her and the Holy spirit came upon her. Then that Holy thing was born of her which was called the Son of God.

Would you bring forth fruit unto God, who once brought forth fruit only unto death? You must become the Bride of Christ. In union with him holy fruitfulness becomes possible. No holy thing can be born of you that is not begotten of him. But in union with Him everything holy becomes as natural and as necessary as in union with sin evil fruitfulness becomes inevitable.

This marital union involves also corresponding *exclusiveness*.

In all our human relations duty and delight keep pace—the higher the privilege and the closer the intimacy the stronger the debt we owe to love and the more exclusive the bond. For example, there are three terms we apply to our relations to others whom we know: acquaintance, friendship, wedded love. Acquaintance is not intimate, and it has no bounds; one may have thousands and tens of thousands of acquaintances. But when acquaintance passes into friendship, the circle narrows and includes fewer persons; and in proportion as the intimacy is closer the number is fewer.

But again the obligation is correspondingly

binding. A man owes little to his acquaintances beyond the courtesies of common life. But to his best friends he owes much, for intimacy and unity are purchased at a costly price. My friend has a right to expect of me and exact from me a peculiar jealousy for his reputation, peculiar devotion to his welfare and happiness, and a peculiar sacredness in guarding what he entrusts to me. But when we come to marriage the union is so close that it narrows down the circle so that it embraces only two within it and can admit no more. Nay, the thought of admitting another is destructive of its purity and perfection. Here the obligation is such that either one would die for the other, interposing the body between the other and any threatened danger.

Now, let us remember that the believer's relation to the Lord Jesus is marital, and its obligations, like its privileges, are marital—the relation is so close it is exclusive—it closes in two parties and closes out all others. No man can serve two masters; but much less can one wife yield herself to two husbands. Any love for another is disloyalty to the lawful spouse, and is known by one of the most offensive words in human language—adultery.

This word when used in scripture and applied to the believer has generally no reference to violations of the *seventh* commandment as such, but of the *first*. When James rebukes adulterers and adulteresses he is referring to those who, while married to Christ, are coquetting with the world that is his enemy; and he says "the friendship of the world is enmity with God."

This passage of scripture, which lifts us to the very summit of exalted privilege, confronts us with the thunders and lightnings of Divine warning. You are permitted to regard yourself as the Bride of Christ. But remember that because you are thus admitted to Bridal union, every act of sin strikes at the very foundation of this union, as adultery strikes at the very basis of marriage. What would you think of a wife who, while calling a man her husband, ventures to see how far she can trifle and flirt and coquette with a betrayer, and yet not lose her husband altogether? and what shall be thought of a believer who ventures to see how far he can dally with the forbidden pleasures of this world and the desires of the flesh, and not altogether forfeit His Saviour?

"Do ye think," adds James, "that the scripture speaketh in vain: The Spirit that dwelleth in us jealously desireth us?" I suppose that somewhat obscure passage means that the Heavenly Bridegroom, now seated on His Father's throne, claims His Bride for Himself and jealously desireth her altogether for Himself. Think of it! God claims and desires you exclusively for His own love, use and delight. That thought ought to make sin impossible, and, so far as it possesses and really controls, it will make sin as unnatural as impurity is to a loyal wife.

The warning may explain what follows in this chapter. We have two unions contrasted here: one with the law, which leaves us to the working of lust and which brings forth only sin; and the other with Christ, which makes love the controlling passion and brings forth fruit in newness of Life. Now, if we mistake not, this much-disputed passage, Rom. vii. 7–25, shows us the believer in his experience of the two conflicting principles at work — Love of God on one hand, lust of flesh on the other hand, contrary the one to the other. Yet even the *regenerate will* is not strong enough to overcome, and Paul cries out, "I approve the law as righteous, holy, perfect, good and spiritual"; but he is not practically delivered from the Power of Evil; and whenever he thinks of his still existing bondage to the old habits and tendencies of the carnal nature, he can only cry out, "O wretched man that I am! Who shall deliver me from the body of this death." But it is not a hopeless cry. He answers, "I thank God, through Jesus Christ, Our Lord!" We all have uttered his cry of despair. How many of us can as confidently use his shout of victory?

The bearing of all this on holiness is perfectly plain. Marriage is the secret of parentage—union with Jesus will in all cases be the secret of holy fruitfulness. While, and so far as, united vitally to Christ, we have power to love and serve and obey God.

A curious illustration of this truth in another sphere was given to me by the Rev. Mr. Devins. At Northfield, at the Auditorium, the reporter of the *New York Tribune* was seeking to transmit, by telegraph, to the paper, one of the addresses there delivered. He found that for some unknown cause the current and circuit were broken—the wire would not work, and this made it necessary to send over to South Vernon and transmit from a new station. The linemen found that the wire at one point near the operator's table had lost its insulation and was touching the ground and discharging its electric power into the earth. What a parable of life! There were men and women in that audience who were in such contact with the world that they could neither contain, retain, nor transmit blessing. If you want Christ-life to become Christ-power, you must maintain separation unto God. The touch of sin is fatal to power.

VI

SPIRITUAL UNION WITH CHRIST

Up to this point there has been no mention of the Holy Spirit in this argument on non-continuance in sin; and, indeed, so far in this epistle the Holy Spirit has been barely referred to twice (i. 4 and v. 6). But when we reach this eighth chapter we find it so full of the Holy Spirit that within these thirty-nine verses He is at least twenty-eight times distinctly mentioned or obviously referred to, and His activities pervade the whole chapter.

It would seem that this must be a very important feature of this part of the great demonstration that to go on sinning is both needless and unbelieving. In the latter part of chapter vii., from verse seven to the close, occurs one of the most difficult and disputed passages in the word of God. Does it refer to the regenerate or unregenerate man? What is the state of this man who delights in the law of God after the inward man, yet finds another law in his members warring against the law of his mind and bringing him into captivity to the law of sin ; who is this that when he would do good finds evil present with him ? etc. I do not hesitate to say that in my own judgment this is a faithful portrait of every child of God, up to the point in his experience where the Spirit of God becomes to him a living, present indwelling and inworking Spirit of power and holiness. And if this be the true interpretation we can understand why this experience of the disciple is brought into the argument at this point. Hitherto the Holy Spirit has been left out of the discussion. We have had the working of the law, the death and resurrection of Christ, the working of faith identifying us with Him, the refusal to yield to sin, and the positive surrender to God, and the believing soul wedded to the Lord Jesus in bridal union in order to bring forth fruit unto God. And yet it is true that, even with the apprehension of all these great facts and truths, the believing soul, feeling the awful power of inborn and inbred sin, finds an inevitable warfare before him, in which the enemy is stronger than himself. How shall all these truths, which he has been taught in these two chapters, about his judicial, vital, practical, actual, marital union with Jesus be made so real to him as to strengthen him with courage for the encounter? How shall the image of his Master and Lord be so kept before him that he shall never lose sight of him ? How shall a new law in his spiritual life assert itself as sufficiently mighty to annul the power of the law of sin and death? At the conclusion of that eighth chapter Paul says, in despair, "O wretched man that I am; who shall deliver me from the body of this death?" He feels like a victim of ancient tyranny, chained to a dead carcase and compelled to drag it about with him, breathe its infection and the taint of corruption, and he despairs of self-deliverance. But despair changes to hope, for he thanks God through Jesus Christ our Lord. For what does he thank God? It seems to me it is for that next and most blessed source of deliverance of whom the eighth chapter is the supreme revelation—the Holy Spirit of God, whom he recognizes as the Divine indwelling Power and Person who accomplishes for the believer these things.

First—He takes of Christ and shows to the believer.

Second—He testifies of Christ to the believer.

Third—He glorifies Christ in the believer.

We shall see what this means, but let it be now said in a word, that upon the Holy Spirit depends wholly the clear, true apprehension of all the facts of Redemption—until He works in us they are fancies or, at best, theories rather than facts. So soon as He practically possesses us we become adjusted to these truths, so that they become actually effective in our daily life.

It cannot be by any accident that this eighth

chapter contains a fuller revelation of the Spirit in His work in the believer than any other in the Epistles; and the bearing of all this teaching on the believer's holy living can be seen only by a careful collation and comparison of the testimony herein contained. Let us take notice of each mention of the Spirit herein found, and of the peculiar and characteristic feature of each separate mention. We pass by that in the first verse, as it is generally regarded as an interpolation, not being found in the best manuscripts.

Verse 2. The law of the *Spirit of life* in Christ Jesus hath made me free from the law of sin and death.

Here is Life in contrast to death; Liberty in contrast to bondage.

4. That the righteousness of the law might be fulfilled in us who *walk* not after the flesh but *after the Spirit.*

Here is a walk after the Spirit — strength in contrast to weakness; obedience in contrast to sin; ability in contrast to disability and inability.

5. They that are after the Spirit do *mind the things of the Spirit.*

Here is a mind of the Spirit in contrast to a mind of the flesh, a habit of thinking, feeling, desiring, loving, choosing spiritual things.

6. To be *spiritually minded is life and peace.*

Here is Life in contrast to death; peace in contrast to alienation ; subjection in contrast to rebellion ; pleasing God instead of enmity.

7. Ye are not in the flesh but *in the Spirit*, if so be that the *Spirit of God dwell in you.*

Here is a mutual abiding—the Spirit in us and we in the Spirit ; language only intelligible when the Spirit is conceived as the *element* in which we live, move, and have our being.

9. Now, if any man *have not the Christ Spirit* he is none of His.

Here is identity with Christ by partaking of his spirit, the one test and proof of being in Christ and His being in us.

10. The *spirit is life* because of Righteousness.

Here is the identity of Life and righteousness, showing what the life of the Spirit is, enabling power to do the will of God.

11. If the *Spirit of Him that raised up Jesus* from the dead dwell in you, He that raised up Jesus from the dead shall also *quicken your mortal bodies by His Spirit* that dwelleth in you.

Here we have the Spirit of Life, the Spirit of Resurrection—imparting His quickening power even to the mortal body (note the distinction between the *mortal* and *corruptible* body, as in 1 Cor. xv.). The mortal body is the living body, liable to death ; the corruptible body is the dead body, already under power of death. The Spirit that dwells in the body exercises even over the body a life-giving and enabling power.

13. If *through the Spirit ye do mortify the deeds of the body* ye shall live.

Here the Spirit is the power that makes *dead* what ought to die, as He makes alive what ought to live.

14. As many as are *led by the Spirit* of God they are the sons of God.

Here the Spirit, who is life and liberty, is also the leader of the child of God. Notice a leader is not one who goes before simply, but who takes us by the hand and insures our following.

15. Ye have received the *Spirit of adoption whereby we cry Abba Father.*

Here the Spirit is the secret of conscious *sonship*, giving us power and right to *address God as Father* in contrast to a servant, who says Master, or a subject, who says Lord—the life of privilege and possession Godwards. Here love as well as faith is traced to the Spirit.

16. The *Spirit himself beareth witness* with our spirit that we are the children of God.

Here we have assurance of sonship by the Spirit, and of heirship and expectancy. All *hope*, as well as faith and love, the fruit of the Spirit.

26. The Spirit also *helpeth our infirmities.*

Here the reference is to our natural ignorance and incapacity to pray aright. We *know not*, etc. The Spirit intercedes in us and for us; our groanings are his movings.

What a body of teaching on the Spirit's relation

to the believer's holiness! To him are here traced Life, Liberty, strength, ability, holy mind, peace, subjection of will, pleasing God, identity with Christ, participation in the nature of God, enabling power, bodily quickening and mortifying, leadership in holiness, conscious sonship and heirship, the filial spirit and the filial tongue, assurance of faith and love and hope, and help in our infirmities, especially in prayer.

These are all the direct references to the Spirit, but every verse in this sublime chapter must be read with Him in it if it is understood.

After examining, one by one, the references to the Spirit which this chapter contains, we cannot avoid the conviction that here is to be found the key to that rapturous shout of thanksgiving in chapter vii. 25. When Paul is at the very verge of the abyss of despair of all self-help or legal sanctification, he cries out "who shall deliver me from the body of this death! I THANK God through Jesus Christ our Lord." And this chapter reveals what was that new truth that was the solution of all his difficulties.

We ought to have no difficulty in *locating* this experience of the apostle if we judge his case by our own. After we have learned what Christ has done for us, and what is our standing before God in him; after we have passed into the regenerate state and our will is to do the will of God, we still find a lack of *power to perform*, and are constantly brought to the verge of despair at our ineffectual efforts.

A glance at the biography of eminent saints will show this as the common experience of believers. They discover a double tendency within them—a tendency downward and a tendency upward. There are two laws—one of gravitation toward Evil, another of gravitation toward God and goodness: may we not say, using scientific terms, a centrifugal and a centripetal force, one of which sways at one time and the other at another. And the problem of the new life is how to ensure the constant sway of the centripetal. There is an honest effort to serve and please God. But the temper is unsanctified, the tongue is untamed, the disposition is tainted with envy and jealousy and malice and uncharitableness.

There is even a deeper difficulty. We notice that in the seventh chapter the *Law* is as prominent as the *Spirit* is in the eighth. In twenty-five verses we find the word law or commandment twenty-eight times and the Spirit not once. Those who construe this experience of Paul as that of an unregenerate man contend that it is unconceivable that he could thus look to the law for *justification* after he was converted. Just so, but may he not be here depicting the conflicts of a man who looks to the law for *sanctification* as the Galatians did?

There is a peril which besets the Saint exactly correspondent with that which besets the Sinner.

The sinner goes about to establish his own justification by a resort to legal works; and when he comes to utter despair of self-help he finds pardon and peace in the finished work of Christ on the Cross. But how often the converted soul, going about to establish his own sanctification, resorts to legal works. After accepting Christ as Saviour, there is a continual temptation to a legal spirit. Every day we are prone to measure our acceptance with God by our measure of faithfulness; what we have done or failed to do, and so we are tossed up and down and driven to and fro by our double mindedness; but from this state of doubt and conflict—this Doubting Castle—there is but one deliverance. We must learn now that the law must be abandoned as our *hope of sanctification* just as it was previously abandoned as our ground of *justification*. Having found peace with God by looking to Christ's finished work *on the cross*, we must now find the peace of God by looking to Christ's finished work *on the throne*, of which the Holy Spirit is both the sign and seal.

After Paul met Christ on the way and learned that in being baptized into Christ he put on Christ and washed away his sins, he doubtless, like his fellow-believers, got into the snare of seeking sanctification by his own efforts, and got his eyes off Jesus, and hence needed this new lesson to learn how to serve God in holiness and righteousness. He had learned how he was alive unto God in Christ; how, as a regenerate man, he had a new Master to serve, a new mould of doctrine to obey from the heart, a new husband to love and submit to as an espoused bride; and now the question arises, how and where shall I find the *enabling power* to do all this? Where is the divine attraction sufficiently mighty to overcome all the yearnings and longings and corrupt tendencies of the flesh in which dwelleth no good thing.

The eighth chapter of Romans is the triumphant answer. In Jesus Christ as Saviour I am justified; through Jesus Christ as Lord I am sanctified. Justified by His death and shed blood, sanctified by His life and Spirit shed forth from heaven, as His blood was shed forth on earth. As there was no solution to the problem of justification without the Death and Resurrection, there is no solution to the problem of justification without His Ascension and Intercession, the immediate fruit and sign of which is the coming of the Holy Spirit to dwell in each believer, and become to him life, liberty, power, strength, and all else needful to victorious life.

This is the germ of thought expanded in the Eighth of Romans, and it is perhaps the *greatest thought ever put before the mind of a believer*, and therefore the most difficult for any carnal mind to take in. By faith I am made one with Christ in this supreme sense: "He that is joined to the Lord is one spirit." 1 Cor. vi. 17. The Holy

Spirit which was in Him the spirit of Life and holiness and resurrection and newness of life, is in me; and what He wrought in Christ, He will work in me just so far as my complete surrender to Him makes it possible. May it be put still more plainly? Faith in Christ's work is indispensable to salvation; faith in the Spirit's work is as indispensable to sanctification—to holiness.

This greatest truth is here presented in many aspects—like a jewel with many faces, each reflecting the light at a new angle and with new colors—for brevity we may select the following:

Three Laws are mentioned:

1. The Law of God—the rule of Duty.
2. The Law of sin and death, a tendency in the carnal man.
3. The Law of the Spirit of Life in Christ Jesus which makes free from the law of sin and death.

The Holy Spirit, a new *mind* or mode of apprehension; a new *law* or tendency; a new *life* or secret of power; a new *element* or sphere of existence.

The Holy Spirit is here presented as the *Complement* to Christ's work; as the new *Element* in which the believer lives: as the *Ligament* of union with Christ.

He is thus the secret of Enablement. The ligament is what makes the joint perfect and holds bone to its socket, and the invisible bond between the believer and Christ, whereby identity is established and unity perfected and ability assured; nay, affinity or like nature and attraction is to be found only in Him.

One of these thoughts is here so conspicuous we may well tarry to consider it. The Holy Spirit is the disciple's *Element*. We use this word, Element, of a simple substance beyond which our analysis cannot go; and because the ancients held that there were four original elements—earth, air, fire and water—these have been commonly known as the four elements. But the word element has been used of the state or sphere of anything, natural to it, suited to its existence; and so we talk of earth as the element of the plant and the worm; of air as the element of bird and insect; of water as the element of the fish and marine plant, and of fire as the element of the Salamander, whose cold body was supposed to be insensible to heat and to have power not only to resist, but overcome it.

The eighth and ninth verses not only suggest an element, but can be understood only as applied to an element. "Ye are not *in* the flesh, but *in the Spirit* if so be that *the Spirit* of God dwell *in you*." Of only one thing can it be said that it is in that which is also in it, *viz.*: an element. The earth is taken up into the plant as the plant is in the earth. The fish is in the water, yet the water is in the fish; the bird is in the air, yet the air is in the bird, and if you put the poker in the fire, the fire is also in the poker, as you find out if you touch it. So the Spirit is the *element* in which the believer lives, moves and has his being.

Now we observe *seven* facts about the elements:

1. Vastness, the element being always greater than all that lives in it, and sufficient for all.
2. Vitality, the element supplying life to that which it contains and sustains.
3. Variety and contrariety, the elements differing and even antagonizing each other.
4. Independence, the element being independent of the animal.
5. Indispensableness, the element being necessary to the animal.
6. Mutuality, the element being in the animal while the animal is in the element.
7. Individuality, each element having its own peculiar conditions, persistence, and resistance to temporary exposure to hostile influence.

All these are applicable to the Spirit of God. He is infinite, while all that live in Him are finite. He is, therefore, larger and greater than all the children of God whom He sustains, and while all may have all there is in Him, none can absorb Him so as to rob any other or diminish aught of the supply.

Again, He is the source of all vitality, the very breath of life, and of all sufficiency to the believer.

Again, there are two elements—the flesh and the Spirit, and these are contrary the one to the other. The worldly man lives in the flesh, and, according to the kind and measure of his life, he thrives in that element. The spiritual man lives in the Spirit and can thrive only in that divine element.

Again, the Holy Spirit is independent of the believer and can exist in all His fulness without him, while He is indispensable to the believer, who cannot exist as such without constant dependence on Him.

Again, there is Mutuality, for it is as true of Him that He dwells in the believer as that the breath is in the body; yet it is equally true that the believer abides in Him, as that the body must abide in the atmosphere in order that the atmosphere may supply new breath at each instant.

And, finally, the Spirit of God has his own conditions. In the world of nature there are amphibious creatures that can live in more than one element, but in God's spiritual realm there are no amphibious beings. True, there may be a temporary departure from the conditions of true life without the utter destruction of that life, as the fish may leap into the air or the bird drop into the water, and each may survive, because it returns to its own element; but to continue in the air is death to the fish, as to continue in the water is death to the bird.

Now, here, if we mistake not, is the most valuable suggestion in all this teaching, for it explains how and why we are sustained in holy living or, on the other hand, commit sin. So long as we keep in the element of the Spirit, how can we intelligently and voluntarily transgress against God? John writes: "He that abideth in Him, sinneth not," *i.e.*, so long and so far as we abide in Him, we are kept from sinning; it is when, so long and so far as we drop into the lower level, and are in the other element of the flesh which stifles our true spiritual life, that we sin. The disciple finds the element of the world, in which the carnal man lives and delights, stifling to his true life; and the worldly man finds the element of the Spirit, if by any means he gets into it, stifling to his worldly life. These are contrary the one to the other, so that ye may not in the element of the Spirit do the things that ye would in the element of the flesh. Gal. v. 17.

The thought I would impress is, that, in all victory over sin, everything depends on maintaining the vigor and vitality of spiritual life by abiding in the Spirit of God, and that the one peril is that we lose the blessed enablement by losing the vitalizing contact.

Here, then, are we to recognize the whole secret of enablement. There is a ligament which unites the believer to Christ and through which the secret of His life and power is communicated to us—our unity being assured with Him and in Him with God. We become partakers of His Spirit, and feel His attraction and affinity Godward working in us. We think as He thinks and love as He loves, and are drawn as He is drawn, from above, not from beneath. Here is enablement, empowerment. The soul born of God hungers and thirsts after God. Like birds which, hatched by an intruder, when they hear the voice of the true mother, fly to her, a soul born of God, hearing His voice, instinctively flies to His wings and takes refuge in His bosom.

VII

ETERNAL UNION WITH CHRIST

Romans viii. 18–39.

Here we reach the fitting climax of this sublime argument, and get the crowning point of prospect. Paul begins at this point to lead his readers to take a wider outlook both into the eternal past and future. Time, with its sufferings and struggles, its temptations and trials, is forgotten in the boundless horizon of God's eternal purpose in Jesus Christ. The transition is not abrupt, but natural; for he has just been referring to the Spirit's co-witness to our sonship and heirship; and, as the *heir looks forward* to an inheritance, a new conception is now introduced.

"This present time" has occupied our attention hitherto : our present identification with Christ by faith as the ground of our resistance to sin and yielding to God, and our present relations to Him as Saviour, Substitute, Master, Lord, Bridegroom, as a preventive against sin, as an incentive to holiness. But now the inspired apostle says: "I reckon that the sufferings of *this present time* are not worthy to be compared with the *glory which shall be revealed in us*"; and from this point the key words are "expectation," "hope," "shall be," "waiting," to be conformed, "redemption," all of which look toward an eternal *future;* or such words as "His purpose," "foreknow," "predestinate," "loved us," which turn our thought back to the eternal *past.* And thus looking back to that love and purpose which had no beginning because before all things; and forward to that final consummation which knows no after disaster, Paul completes his great argument by the rapturous persuasion, that, as there is now no condemnation, there shall be no separation.

When we apply to this aspect of our union with Christ, the word *eternal*, we must first understand the meaning of that grand word. It differs from the words "unending" and "immortal" and "perpetual," for they refer only to the future. For instance, an immortal life is a life that, being begun, has no end, but an eternal life is one which has neither beginning nor end.

How, then, can it be said that the believer has "eternal life," or that his union with Christ is "eternal," when we all have a definite hour of birth, and so of beginning?

Here lies one of God's deep mysteries. When by faith we become united to the Lord, we are considered as sharing His eternal life, as partakers of the Divine nature, and as heirs of God's entire glory—past, present and future. Human illustrations do not reach to the grandeur of this theme, but we may get a glimpse of this mystery through other forms and facts. For example, when you set a scion in a mature tree, and the graft becomes thoroughly incorporated with the new stock, it becomes part of the whole tree, inseparable from it, and in a storm or time of frost or drought, all the strength that is in the tree by reason of age and growth sustains and nourishes the young and feeble graft. The graft shares not the future of that tree's life alone, but all the accumulations of its past also; it becomes identified with the whole history of that tree. When a child is adopted, or, especially, is born into a family, is made or becomes a son and heir, that child becomes also one with the whole history of the family, all its dignity, property, history, its fame and fortune, as well as its name and social standing. It is impossible to draw a line at the point where the new son enters the family, whether by birth or adoption, and separate the previous from the coming history. As far back as the family lineage is traceable, the beginnings of the accumulation of wealth, the starting point in culture and character—from that remote point whatever the family is and represents has been developing, and the new son comes into the inheritance of it all. There is a law of *he-*

redity that looks back, as well as another law of *inheritance*, that looks forward.

The child born by the Spirit into God's family has not only his inheritance, but his heredity. Whatever the family of God means, or includes, it belongs to every child of God. The believer, new born, born from above, made a partaker of the divine nature, becomes also a partaker of the divine history, dignity, possessions, glory. The life before him has no end, and is immortal, but more than this, it has a new quality and character, for immortality is not necessarily a blessing. Eternal life partakes of God's own eternal and unchangeable perfection; it knows neither death nor decay, but is perpetually young, knowing no advance of age, which is a form of decay. Whatever there is in God's eternal past that is beautiful, victorious, glorious, becomes part of every believer's right and privilege and possession.

This part of the epistle can be apprehended only when this sublime idea possesses the mind. Here the august mystery of God's Eternal Purpose in our salvation, sanctification, glorification, is unveiled to our astonished eyes. Believers are described as "the called according to His purpose," and this thought is further expanded till it is unmistakable: "For whom He did foreknow He also did predestinate to be conformed to the image of His Son that He might be the first born among many brethren. Moreover, whom He did predestinate, them He also called, and whom He called, them He also justified, and whom He justified, them He also glorified."

Even a child of God may stumble at this mystery of Election, but that it is *taught* here is unmistakable. Every saved soul must trace salvation, back of all human choice of God, to God's choice of us. There was in God both a foreknowing and a forechoosing, and consequently a foreworking. His was the whole scheme and plan of our salvation. He devised it in the solitudes of eternity, and he wrought it out and is still working it out through the ages. Five distinct stages in the development of this plan of salvation are here named:

Whom he did *forcknow*,
He also did *predestinate*.
He also *called*.
He also *justified*.
He also *glorified*.

One important step seems here omitted.—He also *sanctified*—which in the complete series belongs between the last two, but it is implied in the preceding phrase "to be conformed to the image of his Son."

Now let it be noticed that, from the foreknowing and forechoosing of saved souls, every step, calling, justifying, sanctifying, glorifying, is a step taken by God, rather than by man. What we call saving faith is not an *original* movement toward God but a *responsive* movement to His. Faith chooses God, but in response to His choice of us; faith calls on God, but in response to His calling of us; faith justifies because it accepts His justifying work; faith sanctifies because it surrenders us to His sanctifying spirit; faith brings us to glory, but because it follows Him who prepares the glory for us and leads the way in person to that glory. The one comprehensive thought is that my salvation from first to last is the work of God. It is for me a present salvation having a definite moment of beginning in my acceptance of Christ as Saviour. But for Him it is an eternal salvation: its roots reach down and back to the eternal past of his purpose, and its branches reach up and forward to the flower and fruit of perfection in glory in the future.

Such is the grand conception, and if we seek to know its practical bearing on holiness we have only to follow the apostolic argument. Paul himself asks, "What shall we then say to these things," which is equivalent to asking, What bearing has this truth on noncontinuance in sin? We have only to note the phrases he uses, to see what God's eternal purpose has to do with our holiness.

We select the following conspicuous expressions:

The glory which shall be revealed in us.

The glorious liberty of the children of God.

The adoption, to wit, the redemption of our body.

We are saved by hope.
All things work together for good, etc.
Predestinate to be conformed.
More than conquerors, etc.

Here are *seven* emphatic phrases, but they are only hints of a truth too deep and broad and high for our measurement. The one impression from the whole of the latter half of this chapter is that *our salvation*, with all that *pertains to it*, justification, sanctification, glorification, *is provided for in the changeless purpose of God*. And, therefore, important as are my *will* and *faith* and *obedience* and *conformity*, the grand assurance of my present holiness and final perfection is found in another Will back of mine, prior to it and supreme over it—the Will of God. To yield myself to God is therefore to yoke my impotence to His omnipotence, and to make possible for Him to work in me as only He can work. The more fully, therefore, I trust and entrust myself to Him, the more absolutely and fully will He work in me and through me His perfect work.

This, then, is the grand central thought: Every believer's Life is *a plan of God*, the Father, and hence part of a larger, all-embracing plan of the Trinity. A careful study of the verses, from the sixteenth verse to the thirty-ninth will show that at least *seven* features of this plan are here exhibited, all of them bearing on the question of noncontinuance in sin.

1. ETERNITY.—This plan embraces past, present, and future, and we find here the tenses that correspond to this threefold fact—retrospect, aspect, prospect. There is the past: "Whom He did foreknow He also did predestinate, called, justified." There is the present: We are the children of God; now no condemnation. We suffer with Him the sufferings of this present time; the whole creation groaneth and travaileth in pain together. We ourselves groan within ourselves. The Spirit helpeth our infirmities, maketh intercession for us. We are more than conquerors. There is also the future—if children, then heirs—that we may be glorified together. The glory which shall be revealed in us; the creature itself, also shall be delivered. Waiting for the adoption, to wit: the redemption of our body. What shall separate us? etc.

What a help and joy to know that God loved and chose me long before I loved and chose Him; that He began the good work in me and will continue it until the day of Jesus Christ, and that the perseverance of the saints is the perseverance of God!

This suggests a second prominent feature of God's plan in human salvation:

2. CERTAINTY.—Throughout this chapter there is an air of confident assurance. It begins, "There is therefore now no condemnation;" it ends, "There shall be no separation." It is not a

may be, but a shall be, throughout. Man's plans are always uncertain, for man's will is vacillating and his energy, human, and his power to carry out his own will, finite. But God's Will moves on its changeless course through the ages. Perfect from the beginning, it admits no change, and infinite power assures its execution.

3. UNITY AND UNIVERSALITY.—God's plan is all comprehensive. It embraces all the persons of the Godhead, and all are distinctly mentioned here. We are declared to be sons of God and heirs of God; sons with Christ and heirs with Christ, and both Christ and the Spirit are represented as our Intercessors with the Father.

All believers are embraced in this plan. As many as are led by the Spirit of God are here embraced in the sons of God: "Them that love God and are the called according to his purpose."

"All things" are embraced in God's plan, and this phrase is used here in two widely different senses. In verse 28 it means all the varied occurrences and experiences of life. In verse 32 it refers to the varied bestowments and endowments of grace. God's plan leaves nothing out. All things work, and work together for good—all things, even trials, at which we murmur and complain. The storms which threaten to uproot the trees really root them more firmly and deeply in the soil. The blows which one might think would make the cast-iron brittle, really cause it to undergo a sort of cold annealing and increase its strength and tenacity. The enforced rest of sorrow and pain, sickness and disappointment, John Ruskin compares to the rest in which there is no music, but the making of music; not the end of the tune, but a pause in the choral hymn of our lives, during which the divine musician beats the time with unvarying count, catching up the next note as if no breaking-place had come between.

God's plan includes all our temptations. There is a divine philosophy of evil, and it is made to work good. Temptation has its holy office, its benign purpose. It tests us, and so attests us; it strengthens by revealing our weakness and so the source of our true strength, and it actually uplifts and sanctifies by teaching us how to resist and overcome. Blessed is the man that endureth temptation, for when he is tried and proved, he shall receive the crown of life, the prize of the victorious soul.

God's plan includes the whole creation which shared the curse of the fall and must share the blessing of the Redemption; and hence the whole material creation is represented as groaning and travailing in pain, like a woman with child, waiting for that new creature that is brought forth only through such travail.

God's plan is like a vast universal mechanism that fills the universe and embraces all things. He who loves God, and is led by His Spirit, comes into that plan as a wheel into a perfect machine, and henceforth he is a part of God's universal harmony and system, all "circumstances" being embraced.

4. SAFETY AND SECURITY.—If God be for us who can be against us. There can be no successful *opposition*. What shall separate us? There can be no real *separation*. When once in such a system, there can be no *collision*, for every part of this perfect mechanism has its definite place and sphere of revolution, and interference cannot be imagined, for divine forethought and wisdom are behind all things. Nor can there be any separation, for that would imply breakage and disaster.

5. SANCTITY.—We are predestinated to be conformed to the image of His Son. However strong and whole hearted my purpose to be the Lord's, my dependence is on a Higher will. We have seen how the apostle depicts the heroic but unsuccessful conflict of the regenerate man, with the old man of sin, before he appreciates the power of the indwelling, inworking Spirit of God; but now we see the will of God reinforcing and strengthening the will of man.

Let us borrow an illustration from common life. A man in New England has a mill, whose wheel depends for motion on a small and irregular water supply; but he tapped a river near by, and so got an unfailing stream at his disposal. We need to tap the river of God and have His will energize our own.

6. VICTORY.—We are more than conquerors. How is that possible? That expression is used only here, and where can be found a more significant one. What is this more than conquest?

(*a*) He is more than conqueror who organizes victory, not out of conquest but out of *defeat*.

(*b*) He is more than conqueror who not only vanquishes the foe but *makes foes his tributaries and allies*.

(*c*) He is more than conqueror who is not only victor in the fight, but who conquers *without fighting*.

(*d*) He is more than conqueror who never knows *even the fear of the foe*, but whose hope and faith are victors in advance.

A true child of God is thus, in every sense, a more than conqueror. God is with him and none can be against him and succeed. He organizes victory out of defeat. As Christ died, but in dying brought deliverance from death, the child of God dies to live, and in death triumphs over death. Hear Paul: "For thy sake we are killed all the day long"—a perpetual dying, and that dying a victory over self and Satan. He loses life to find it; he is buried as a seed, but the harvest comes up from the burial.

The disciple turns his foes into his friends. The trials and temptations that seem to threaten his peace and his power and even his final perfection, are the means of promoting them. What the Devil means to use as a messenger of Satan to buffet him, becomes the means of a revelation of the infinite strength made perfect in weakness. The circumstances which, when they come between us and God, eclipse Him, when they are seen in the light of God's plan become an additional cause of our thanksgiving, luminous with his purpose.

The disciple conquers without fighting. He stands still to see the salvation of God. He abandons effort to rest on the finished work of God. And so confident is he of victory that he gives thanks in advance for a triumph that is so sure that before the battle the song of victory is in his mouth.

This eighth chapter of Romans has a sweet word for the Christian disciple on this subject of victory.

Who shall lay anything to the charge of God's Elect? Verses 33-39. We too often pass carelessly over these words, without noticing their comprehensiveness.

Three great questions are asked and each has reference to a different class of foes:

"Who shall lay anything to the charge of God's elect?"

"Who is he that condemneth?"

"Who shall separate us from the love of Christ?"

In all these questions the pronoun is masculine, implying a *person* or at least a personification.

The Person who brings charge against God's Elect is Satan, the *accuser* of the brethren. But we are not to be afraid of his accusation, however founded upon the facts of our unbelief and unfaithfulness. For we have in God our Justifier.

He that condemns is the *Law*, which is in this passage personified, as compelled to accuse and condemn. But, while justly condemned by the law, there is an atonement all-sufficient to expiate guilt of past sin and an advocate all-sufficient to meet the present and future needs of a forgiven soul.

The separating barriers between us and God are here personified and enumerated, and they are, first seven and then ten, making seventeen in all—tribulation, distress, etc.—study the seventeen and you will find nothing left out. Love triumphs over all. Tribulation, love uses to refine and purify; distress, love uses to bring us closer; persecution becomes by love a test of love, and its witness; famine and nakedness, peril and sword only teach us our true satisfaction and security in God. Death only brings the beloved together; even the demons, from the fallen archangel down, are under control of Him who is exalted above every name that is named.

7. GLORY, which shall be revealed, includes :
1. Partaking of the Divine Nature—sympathy with holiness, antipathy against evil.
2. Divine perfection.
3. Divine bliss—character and condition harmonious.

We have thus outlined this great argument, but it is only an outline. God is challenging every believer *not to go on sinning*, and the challenge is based upon the believer's union with Christ, which is manifold in its aspects, and almighty in its power.

We can only say, as we conclude, that it is a master device of Satan to blind our eyes to the true nature and possibilities of our identification with the son of God, and so to prevent our knowing, claiming, and enjoying all its benefits. John Huss, when talking to his friend in prison at Constance, about a dream he had, of the Pope and his bishops trying to efface an image of Christ on the walls of his cell, being advised to let alone his dreams and prepare for his defence, replied—" I am no dreamer : that image of Christ will never be effaced ; it will be painted afresh in all hearts by much better preachers than myself, *and I, awaking from the dead and rising from the grave, shall leap with great joy.*" Even Pope Adrian, the only really earnest Pope of that day, said to the Diet of Nürnberg (1523), "*The heretics Huss and Jerome are now alive again in the person of Martin*

Luther." What if the image of Christ as the Believer's Substitute and Surety could be ineffaceably impressed on the very tablets of our being! How would He who rose from the dead, live again in the person of the believing saint, and a new triumph over sin, death, and Hell!

PUBLICATIONS OF
THE BAKER & TAYLOR CO.,
Publishers and Booksellers,
5 and 7 EAST SIXTEENTH ST., NEW YORK.

ARTHUR T. PIERSON'S WORKS.

THE NEW ACTS OF THE APOSTLES; or, THE MARVELS OF MODERN MISSIONS. A series of lectures upon the foundation of the "Duff Missionary Lectureship," delivered in Scotland, in February and March, 1893, with a chromo-lithographic map of the world, and chart, which show the prevailing religions of the world, their comparative areas, and the progress of evangelization. By Rev. ARTHUR T. PIERSON, D.D., with an introduction by Rev. ANDREW THOMSON, D.D., F.R.S.E., Edinburgh, Scotland. Crown 8vo, cloth, $1.50.

"It may well be doubted whether a more available book on Missions has been published in our time. Nowhere else in four hundred and thirty pages—unless it be in the New Testament—can a pastor, or a leader of monthly concerts and other missionary meetings, find more valuable material in terse and compact form than in this volume."—*Rev. F. F. Ellinwood, D.D., Sec. Presbyterian Bd. of Foreign Missions.*

"The book is a *thesaurus* in the hands of faithful servants of the Lord, second only to the inspired Record, which with zeal and jealousy it honors. The copious and exact index appended will increase the facility with which all students of missions can draw from this most opulent volume the needful information to equip them for active and successful service."—*Rev. Henry M. Parsons, D.D., Toronto, Canada.*

"The volume contains a connected history of the modern missionary movement, skilfully, graphically, and eloquently presented. It is a notable contribution to missionary literature."—*Chicago Advance.*

"The map, the most complete thing of the kind ever published, will be found of great value to students of mission and missionary work. As to the text, perhaps no living author has more carefully studied every feature of mission work and is better fitted to give an intelligent opinion than Dr. Pierson."—*Chicago Inter-Ocean.*

Sent, postpaid, on receipt of the price, by
THE BAKER & TAYLOR CO., Publishers,
5 & 7 East Sixteenth St., New York.

BOOKS BY REV. ARTHUR T. PIERSON, D.D.—(Continued.)

THE DIVINE ENTERPRISE OF MISSIONS. 16mo, cloth, gilt top, $1.25.

In this work the author seeks the eternal and immutable principles of mission work in the utterances of the Master himself. The subject is treated under the Divine Thought, Plan, Work, Spirit, Force, Fruit, and Challenge of Missions.

"Dr. Pierson has come into the very front rank, if he does not actually occupy a position in advance of all other agitators for Foreign Mission work. We know of no other source where broader views or truer stimulus can be found for this greatest work of the Church."—*N. Y. Christian Advocate.*

THE ONE GOSPEL; OR THE COMBINATION OF THE NARRATIVES OF THE FOUR EVANGELISTS IN ONE COMPLETE RECORD. Edited by ARTHUR T. PIERSON. 12mo, flexible cloth, red edges, 75 cents; limp morocco, full gilt, $2.00.

Without taking the place of the four Gospels, this book will be an aid in their study—a commentary wholly biblical, whereby the reader may, at one view, see the complete and harmonious testimony of four independent witnesses.

STUMBLING-STONES REMOVED FROM THE WORD OF GOD. 18mo, cloth, 50 cents.

In this little book many supposed difficulties of the Bible are shown not to be such in fact, and such simple rules of interpretation of a general character are laid down, as to make clear the literal truth of many passages which to some minds have previously been doubtful or only capable of the explanation that they were used metaphorically.

"A little volume worth its weight in gold, in which many of the difficult and obscure passages of Scripture are made clear and easy to be understood."—*Christian at Work.*

"This is a small book, but it contains a good deal—removing many supposed difficulties from the Bible, and helping believers to a better understanding of the book."—*Presbyterian Observer.*

Sent, postpaid, on receipt of the price, by

THE BAKER & TAYLOR CO., PUBLISHERS,
5 AND 7 EAST SIXTEENTH ST., NEW YORK.

BAKER & TAYLOR CO.'S PUBLICATIONS.

TWO BOOKS BY REV. DR. PIERSON.

EVANGELISTIC WORK IN PRINCIPLE AND PRACTICE. By Arthur T. Pierson. 16mo, paper, 35 cents; cloth, $1.25.

An able discussion of the best methods of evangelization by an acknowledged master of the subject.

"If our pen could become as fervent as fire, and as fluent as the wave, we could not write either too warmly or too well of this book. Dr. Pierson has given us a real book—a thunderbolt—a cataract of fire. These flame-flakes ought to fall in showers all over Christendom, and set every house on fire."—*Spurgeon*.

"The book tingles with the evangelistic spirit, and is full of arousement without sliding into fanaticism."—*Springfield Republican*.

"A stirring trumpet-blast to every earnest soul it reaches."—*Christian at Work*.

"Every page is filled with the evangelistic spirit. . . . Dr. Pierson is full of facts, arguments, incidents, illustrations, and pours them over his pages in a molten stream."—*N. Y. Evangelist*.

LOVE IN WRATH; or, The Perfection of God's Judgments. An Address before the Mildmay Conference, London, Eng. By Arthur T. Pierson. Leatherette, gilt top, 35 cents.

This interesting theme is graphically treated by Dr. Pierson under the captions: I. The Judge; II. The Court; III. The Judgment; IV. The Execution; V. The Judged.

"This is one of the best volumes which has come from the hands of Dr. Pierson. In this day, when religion is so apt to be regarded as a sentiment, it is refreshing to have one come out so plainly upon the subject which Dr. Pierson treats. His discussion is admirable. He presents arguments and draws conclusions which cannot be refuted, and which show how the superintending and superabounding love of God is manifested in his judgments."—*Central Baptist*.

Sent, postpaid, on receipt of the price, by

THE BAKER & TAYLOR CO., Publishers,
5 and 7 East Sixteenth St., New York.

BAKER & TAYLOR CO.'S PUBLICATIONS.

SERMONS BY THREE FAMOUS PREACHERS.

STIRRING THE EAGLE'S NEST, and OTHER PRACTICAL DISCOURSES. By Rev. THEODORE L. CUYLER, D.D. 12mo, cloth, with a photogravure portrait of the author, $1.25.

A collection of eighteen sermons thoroughly representative of the author's characteristic style and speech.

"In this volume we have this great Presbyterian divine, whose name has deservedly become a household word in America, at his best. They are strong, clear, spiritual, helpful."—*Boston Traveller.*

"It is such sermons as these that are worth publishing and have a permanent value."—*Presbyterian Journal.*

THE HEART OF THE GOSPEL. Twelve Sermons, delivered at the Metropolitan Tabernacle, London, England. By ARTHUR T. PIERSON. 16mo, cloth, gilt top, $1.25.

"They stand as examples of Dr. Pierson's conspicuous ability as an extempore speaker. The sermons ring out the good old Gospel in sweet clarion tones. There is no uncertainty as to their doctrinal orthodoxy, nor is there any lack of adaptation in them for winning souls."—*N. Y. Observer.*

MILK AND MEAT. Twenty-four Sermons. By Rev. A. C. DIXON, D.D., Pastor of the Hanson Place Baptist Church, Brooklyn, N. Y. 12mo, cloth, $1.25.

These discourses which have been delivered to very large and enthusiastic audiences, seek in book form a still wider hearing. The author's nervous, energetic, and picturesque style of exposition gives his spoken and written words an unflagging interest, which holds the auditor and reader to the end. Aptness of illustration and pointed and forceful presentation characterize the book: while avoiding the grotesque, it is thoroughly popular, entertaining, and natural.

Sent, postpaid, on receipt of the price, by

THE BAKER & TAYLOR CO., PUBLISHERS.

BAKER & TAYLOR CO.'S PUBLICATIONS.

THREE STANDARD BOOKS ON MISSIONS.

THE CRISIS OF MISSIONS; OR, THE VOICE OUT OF THE CLOUD. By ARTHUR T. PIERSON. Paper, 35 cents; cloth, $1.25.

"One of the most important books to the Cause of Foreign Missions—and through them to Home Missions also—whichever has been written. It should be in every library and every household. It should be read, studied, taken to heart, and prayed over."—*Congregationalist.*

THE DIVINE ENTERPRISE OF MISSIONS. A Series of Lectures delivered at New Brunswick, N. J., before the Theological Seminary of the Reformed Church in America upon the "Graves" Foundation in 1891. By Rev. ARTHUR T. PIERSON, D.D. 16mo, cloth, gilt top, $1.25.

"The book is thick-sown with striking illustrations, rich in the lore of missionary heroism, burning with love for souls, fresh and vigorous in its exposition of Scripture. Nowhere have we seen a more stirring presentation of the Christian's function of co-working, co-suffering, co-witnessing with the Triune God."—*Post-Graduate and Wooster Quarterly.*

THE GREAT VALUE AND SUCCESS OF FOREIGN MISSIONS. Proved by distinguished witnesses. By Rev. JOHN LIGGINS, with an Introduction by Rev. ARTHUR T. PIERSON, D.D. 12mo, 249 pages; paper, 35 cents; cloth, 75 cents.

A powerful presentation of overwhelming evidence from independent sources, largely that of Diplomatic Ministers, Viceroys, Governors, Military and Naval Officers, Consuls, Scientific and other Travellers in Heathen and Mohammedan countries, and in India and the British Colonies. It also contains leading facts and late statistics of the missions.

"A grand and irrefutable reply to those who are fond of decrying missions."—*Christian at Work.*

"An overwhelming mass of testimony."—*Springfield Republican.*

Sent, postpaid, on receipt of the price, by
THE BAKER & TAYLOR CO., PUBLISHERS,
5 AND 7 EAST SIXTEENTH ST., NEW YORK.

BAKER & TAYLOR CO.'S PUBLICATIONS.

THREE PULPIT AND PASTORATE BOOKS.

THE DIVINE ART OF PREACHING. By Rev. Arthur T. Pierson, D.D.

Contents.—I. The Sermon as an Intellectual Product. II. The Preacher among His Books III. The Preacher with His Themes. IV. The Preacher Training His Memory. V. The Twin-Laws of the Sermon. VI. Types of Sermon Structure. VII. The Preacher among the Mysteries. VIII. The Preacher among the Critics. IX. The Preacher with His Bible. X. The Preacher in His Pulpit. XI. The Preacher among Snares. XII. The Preacher among His People. XIII. The Preacher Communing with the Spirit.

"It contains the freshest thoughts of one of the leading preachers of the world, on a subject of deep interest to ministers everywhere."—*Cumberland Presbyterian.*

HOW TO BE A PASTOR. By Rev. Theodore Cuyler, D.D.

Contents.—I. Importance of Pastoral Labor. II. Pastoral Visits. III. Visitation of the Sick—Funeral Services. IV. Treatment of the Troubled. V. How to Have a Working Church. VI. Training Converts. VII. Prayer-meetings. VIII. A Model Prayer-meeting. IX. Revivals. X. Drawing the Bow at a Venture. XI. Where to be a Pastor. XII. Joys of the Christian Ministry.

"The fruit of large native sense, long experience, wide observation, and devout consecration."—*Congregationalist.*

THE WORKING CHURCH. By Rev. Charles F. Thwing, D.D.

I. The Church and the Pastor. II. The Character of Church Work. III. The Worth and Worthlessness of Methods. IV. Among the Children. V. Among the Young People. VI. Among Business Men. VII. From the Business Point of View. VIII. Two Special Agencies. IX. The Treatment of Strangers X. The Unchurched. XI. Duties Towards Benevolence. XII. The Rewards of Christian Work. XIII. In the Country Town.

"Every chapter is full of pith, bristling with points, wise, sound, and practical."—*The Evangelist.*

16mo, cloth, gilt top. In a set, $2.25. Separately, each, 75 cents. *Sent, postpaid, on receipt of the price, by*

THE BAKER & TAYLOR CO., Publishers,
5 and 7 East Sixteenth St., New York.

www.ingramcontent.com/pod-product-compliance
Lightning Source LLC
Chambersburg PA
CBHW020119170426
43199CB00009B/565